Beginnings

Also available
by Lindsey Elder
from Alyson Books

Early Embraces

Beginnings

Lesbians talk about the first time
they met their long-term partner

edited by

Lindsey Elder

alyson
books

LOS ANGELES • NEW YORK

MANUFACTURED IN THE UNITED STATES OF AMERICA.

THIS TRADE PAPERBACK ORIGINAL IS PUBLISHED BY ALYSON PUBLICATIONS INC.,

P.O. BOX 4371, LOS ANGELES, CALIFORNIA 90078-4371.

DISTRIBUTION IN THE UNITED KINGDOM BY TURNAROUND PUBLISHER SERVICES LTD.,

UNIT 3 OLYMPIA TRADING ESTATE, COBURG ROAD, WOOD GREEN,

LONDON N22 6TZ ENGLAND.

FIRST EDITION: APRIL 1998

02 01 00 99   10 9 8 7 6 5 4 3 2

ISBN 1-55583-427-2

LIBRARY OF CONGRESS CATALOGING-IN-PUBLICATION DATA

    BEGINNINGS : LESBIANS TALK ABOUT THE FIRST TIME THEY MET THEIR LONG-TERM
    PARTNER / EDITED BY LINDSEY ELDER. — 1ST ED.

      ISBN 1-55583-427-2

      I. LESBIAN COUPLES—UNITED STATES. 2. MATE SELECTION—UNITED STATES.

    I. ELDER, LINDSEY.

    HQ75.6.85B44 1998

    306.76'63—DC21   98-5884 CIP

Contents

PART I Beginnings...

PART II SHE SAID, SHE SAID

Part 1
Beginnings...

Discovery Retold

BY FRANCI MCMAHON

I searched for high lonely meadows
snowy peaks and flint-bedded creeks
where wind would wash me
and hold me in a loose corral.

Instead I found you
a mossy green valley
with snow in your hair
and crevasses running near your eyes.

Your face familiar as a view from a favorite
window, sun and moon in the expected places
seasons rolling by, the same doe
sometimes with twins, crossing the frame.

The lupine, blooming fresh colors every
year from the same corner of the garden.
A stone turned in my hand so often
its whorls a fingerprint on my memory.

You are blue limitless air
the echoing edge of a night cry.
The print of a hard-walled hoof
on a pine needle trail, wild and beckoning.

One Purple Kiss

BY JULES TORTI

And so the story begins with one purple kiss…

I stood naked, despite being fully clothed. My heart pounded like a team of wild horses racing across the savanna. My palms were clammy, my armpits sweaty, and my tongue felt fat and swollen in my mouth. Words seemed unfathomable at that moment. My knees buckled with skyrocketing estrogen levels. Wow. She had the most beautiful eyes.

She was the one; I knew this instantly. It was like the first time I saw the Grand Canyon—that incredible overwhelming feeling of awe. That's how I felt with her. Between us it was spontaneous combustion. We had known each other for years, and then one day, *blamo!* It happened. It was as if we had sipped some secret love potion and fell, mesmerized, into a lover's trance. Our hearts consumed by an innocent kiss. One purple kiss…

Kate and I had not seen each other for months and decided to meet at an AIDS fund-raiser in town. Immediately on finding each other, we embraced, and she kissed me, leaving a little purple smudge on my cheek from her zinced lips. Something had definitely changed between us. We Rollerbladed for hours, oblivious to the distance we covered. I could feel her eyes undressing me and mine undressing her. We finished the course, breathless…from anticipation?

"Let's go get some wings and beer," she suggested.

We opted to go to the Sub Tub. The place was a dive, a very redneck bar. It smelled like stale cigarette smoke, fried onions, and Old Spice—but it served great barbecue wings. The crowd was predictable: a bunch of drunken Sub Tub baseball players stuffed into too-small uniforms that constricted their chubby beer-and-french-fry-enhanced stomachs. I sipped my beer, sitting across from Kate, distracted, almost unaware that anyone else was in the bar with us. Her smile was perfect.

Poking pieces of celery and carrot into a plastic container of blue cheese dip, we carefully avoided eye contact. Kate's partner, Jan, was now sitting on the stool beside her. Was our attraction to each other noticeable? I smiled shyly when our carrots accidentally bumped together in the dip. The emotions we felt were undeniable. I wiped the condensation off the side of my beer bottle with one finger. This wasn't supposed to happen. We were old friends. Kate had a lover. Regardless, I felt myself leaping into the canyon, headfirst. No inhibitions. Reassuring myself that these emotions were innocent.

While crunching on a celery stick, Kate excitedly talked about the upcoming Mudcat Festival in her hometown of Dunnville.

"Mudcats are catfish," she explained. "Dunnville celebrates in good fashion with a fishing derby, a fish fry, fireworks, and a dance at the local fire hall. Do you have any plans for the following weekend?" Her beautiful eyes rested on me.

I was scheduled to work, but my vocal vulva was screaming, *No! You don't have any plans!* Calmly I replied, "No, I don't have any plans."

Kate and I had partied before without Jan around, and that's what we planned to do at the Mudcat. Jan was vacationing up north that weekend at a colleague's cottage. She wasn't at all suspicious of Kate's motives in inviting me to the festival. I wasn't suspicious either, yet a part of me, the part diving headlong into the canyon, knew what was going to happen. On Saturday night Kate was having a barbecue with a bunch of her baseball friends, but what about Friday night? Kate was listening to her vocal vulva as well.

I cycled to Dunnville on Friday afternoon with no intention or expectations of sleeping with Kate. Yeah, I would jump at the chance—but realistically, I never thought I would have the opportunity. She was with Jan. They had been together for 13 years. I pedaled up the driveway, sweaty and exhausted. Kate was relaxing on the back deck, awaiting my arrival. Gratefully I accepted a cold beverage and joined her on the lounge, sinking my tired body into its comfort before having a shower.

When I reappeared from the bathroom, after my shower, I was surprised to find the dining table set for a candlelight dinner. Kate smiled from the kitchen as she stirred the bubbling pasta sauce. Uh-oh. I was seduced already. All she had to do was smile. An open bottle of red zinfandel sat on the counter and I eagerly poured two glasses, thirsty from anticipation. What was I anticipating? Nothing before. But now? We made a toast to the Mudcat Festival, and enjoyed the eye contact we tried to hide at the Sub Tub.

During dinner, before my first mouthful of gnocchi, I felt a warm hand gingerly touch my inner thigh. I took a deep breath, resisting the urge to touch her, everywhere. The Grand Canyon feeling returned. *Was* I standing a little close to the edge? I knew the risk...I knew the danger. I wanted to jump.

My body responded to her touch. Excited endorphins coursed through my veins, my heart pumped hard, my breath was fast and shallow. I hardly remember eating; my body was just going through the motions. Yes, I had left my inhibitions somewhere. Somewhere far from here. Jan was nonexistent.

We left our plates on the table and moved into the living room. Blond hair, blue eyes, golden skin. Reminding myself to breathe, I sat at the opposite end of the couch. Muscular legs, strong arms, firm breasts. She gave me a come-closer look. Suddenly the cat had my tongue. I had butterflies in my stomach. A frog in my throat. And the cow jumped over the moon. I watched as she slid surreptitiously in my direction.

We kissed...tentatively. Soft, gentle, tender. Then, uncontrollably. Her passionate kisses transformed me into a blabbering fool, weakened by rubbery legs wobbling with desire. Whispered honeyed words, an amorous pursuit. I was captivated, conquered. She smiled and caressed my cheek. We had fallen in love over chicken wings and blue cheese dip, consumed by the innocence of one purple kiss.

And so the story continues...

The Surf Maid's Promise

BY RITA M. SCHIANO

I am sitting in the Family Surgical Lounge of St. Vincent's Hospital, waiting. My feet are resting on the edge of a coffee table strewn with today's edition of the Worcester *Telegram & Gazette* and outdated issues of *People*, *Time*, and *Newsweek*. The magazines belong to the hospital staff, I think, because mailing labels are noticeably torn off, or are colored over with a black marker. I hear the metal door bang open, hear the high-pitched squeal of a gurney as it rolls down the short hallway. And as it passes the lounge, I see the familiar black hair. Suddenly I am back in time…

I am sitting in the dormitory lounge at Pettibone House, reading. My feet are resting on the edge of a coffee table strewn with a red-covered five-subject notebook and a worn copy of Plato's *Theory of Knowledge*. I hear the front door creak open, hear footsteps shuffling down the short hallway. And as you turn and walk down the hallway that leads to your room, I see your long black hair, cascading down your shoulders, embracing your tiny waist, resting on your small, shapely buttocks like thousands of fingers.

I watch as you unlock the tall beige wooden door and then disappear into your room. Although your room is next to mine, I rarely see you, never speak to you. I just watch you come and go, and I long to run my fingers through your thick black hair.

Pushing off the brown leather couch in the Family Surgical Lounge, I hurry down the hallway to your hospital room. I stroke the top of your head. Your eyes open; glazed onyx orbs.

"It hurts," you whisper.

I kiss your forehead, as I have done thousands of times over the past 14 years. "I know, honey," I say softly. "Just sleep for now."

We finally speak to each other on the last day of the semester. I knock on your door.

"Who is it?" you call out.

"It's Rita, from next door." My voice sounds hoarse—not because I am ill. I am nervous.

The door opens, and you step out into the hall.

"Um, hi…" I stutter. "I saw a notice on the bulletin board. You're selling your tennis racket?"

"Yeah," you say, eyeing me. "You can check it out, but I think the grip might be wrong for you."

You go back into your room, leaving me standing in the hallway, returning seconds later with a wooden Wilson tennis racket.

"Here, try it." You hand the racket to me.

I grasp the handle, swing it back and forth.

"Do you play tennis?" you ask, suppressing a smile.

"Well, no…not really." I look down at you. You are petite, with skin tanned the color of cinnamon from growing up in Hawaii.

Grabbing the racket from me, you comment, "This isn't right for you. It's too short and the grip is too small." Then, taking my hand, you place yours upon it, palm to palm. "Your hands are much larger than mine. You need a bigger grip."

I am holding your hand when Dr. Riso enters. "I wish I had better news for you, Kay." You squeeze my hand and it feels smaller than usual. "It's malignant. We'll need to schedule the mastecto-my. I'd suggest waiting two weeks to give you time to heal from the biopsy."

Six years pass until we speak again. I am living in New York City, earning a meager living as a jazz singer in nightclubs. I call my college friend, Claire, and invite her to attend my show at an East Side club called Something Different. After the show, I seek out Claire. She is not alone.

"You remember Kay, don't you? Class of '76?" says Claire.

I offer my hand to you. "Yes, of course I do. We lived next to each other at Pettibone my junior year."

You take my hand, squeezing it gently. "Ever get a tennis racket?"

I smile shyly, secretly thrilled that you remember that brief conversation we exchanged over six years ago.

"No, I never did," I tell you.

I join you and Claire for a drink. I notice that you haven't changed much, though your skin is less tanned and your long mane is permed, giving you a wild, rock-and-roll star look, especially in those tight black jeans and black silk baseball jacket. Although it is nighttime, you wear sunglasses.

"I bet people mistake you for Yoko Ono," I say.

"They do." You smile. "But I'm much prettier, don't you think?"

"So what do you think?" you ask me.

Blinking, I say, "I'm sorry. What did you say?"

"I said, what do you think? About the mastectomy? Do you think I'm making the right decision?"

I sit down on the bed and take your hand, although what I really want to do is crawl in next to you, hold you close, take this disease away from you, make you better, make you not have to lose your breast, your hair.

Nodding my head, I say, "Yes, I do. If losing a breast means saving your life, then do it." I try to keep the fear and sadness out of my voice. Your tender look tells me I am not successful.

A nurse comes in carrying a tray with a small container of orange juice and a bowl of strawberry Jell-O. She leaves it on the bed stand.

I fill the plastic cup halfway and hand it to you. As you sip the juice, our eyes meet.

"Don't worry, Rita. If anything happens we'll find each other again. The SurfMaid promised."

We have our first official date on July 3, 1983. You take me to see your favorite movie, *Diva*, then to dinner. I have Thai food for the first time. We spend the evening walking the streets of Greenwich Village, occasionally stopping in a bar for a drink.

It is 1 A.M., and we are at the SurfMaid. The bar is almost empty. Small wooden tables with rickety wooden chairs from some old grade school dot the room; church pews line the walls banquette-style. A large wooden figurehead of a mermaid, its gold and blue paint weathered from years at sea, hangs on the wall. Carved underneath her breasts are the words THE SURFMAID.

We take a table near the jukebox, under the watchful eyes of the SurfMaid. You order a beer; I have Chardonnay.

"Do you have a quarter?" you ask.

Pulling change from my front pocket, I hand one to you. You practically skip to the jukebox, make a selection, and return to the table just as the waiter deposits our drinks. In the background Marvin Gaye croons, "Ooh, baby…when I get this feeling I need sexual healing…come on, come on…Ooh, baby…."

At that moment our eyes meet and linger. I can no longer hear Marvin's sensuous voice. Only the roar of the sea fills my head. Images of past lifetimes with you flash before my eyes like a

Movieola. And even more incredibly, as we walk to my uptown apartment that night, you tell me you had the same experience.

I take your hand, help you from the hospital bed, help you put on the loose button-down flannel shirt. You ease your left arm into the sleeve, wincing from the pain of the biopsy incision. Gently I hold you to me. Your head rests against my shoulder.

I think about the SurfMaid—how that goddess of the sea watched over us that night, two souls who grew up oceans apart, and I am thankful for the gift we were given. Thankful for the moment when we looked into each other's eyes, into each other's soul— suspended in time.

Barbie Dolls, Red Wine, and k.d. lang

BY SONIA ABEL

Wanted: An open-minded, artistic female...

When people ask how Renae and I met, I can't resist jokingly referring to the ad I placed in a local paper. After some surprised and amused looks I confess the ad was for a housemate, not a lover. It was during my college days in Athens, Georgia. My friend Darcy and I needed a third roommate for the three bedroom house we were renting. The first time I saw Renae I thought she was beautiful and obviously a lesbian. I thought it was the Gap clothes (men's, of course), the baseball cap, and Doc Marten shoes that gave her away. Many college students dressed that way, so it must have been her androgynous strut and the way she confidently strolled up to the house on her mountain bike. A few days later she moved in. As she unpacked her car, I couldn't resist a peek at her choice in books. Along with feminist texts there were several environmental books and field guides. Ah, we have a mutual interest in nature, I thought. That's when the crush began.

I'd never dated a woman before. At the time, I was going back and forth between two male lovers, but I have always been attracted to females. Like many women, my first sexual experience was with a girl. Our mothers were friends and we stayed together quite often in the summer. I was nine, she was seven. We watched sexually charged soap operas and played Barbie dolls while our mothers were at work. We didn't have a Ken doll so the ugliest Barbie would play the man. That is until we found my mother's sex manual and found out what a lesbian was. Then our Barbies could just be lesbians. As many curious kids did, we began with back scratches at night and eventually tried everything in the sex manual. We even found her mother's "muscle massager" and experienced prepubescent orgasm, or something close to it. This went on for years until I realized the pleasures I was giving were rarely reciprocated and we were getting too old to call it childhood experimentation anymore.

I didn't think seriously about pursuing my attraction for women until I met Renae. I told her about my childhood same-sex play, and with the help of red wine confessed my lingering attraction to women…and to her. She was stunned by my directness and too shy to reply. I told her I felt we had known each other before. Maybe as Bohemian lovers in a 1920s Parisian bordello. Although she never considered reincarnation, she was flattered and entertained by my musings.

Journal Entry: 7/27/92

Is it a yearning for the unknown? An attraction so great it could never have been felt before? I listen, but mostly I watch—the delicate overbite, the relaxed full lips. I long to touch her so much more than I do, but would these thoughts of her cease if my fantasy became real?

One day when she leaned over to pick something up, I delightfully got a peek at her bare breasts. I tried to keep a straight face as we continued our conversation, and then, as if she knew I was looking, she leaned over a second time in case I didn't get a good look the first. I was deeply in lust.

Renae spoke quite often about feminism and encouraged me to take women's studies. Her passion and intelligence amazed me and made me fall for her even harder. She had such a warm, disarming personality, and we began to open up to each other on a deeper level. I confided in her about the sexual molestation I had endured as a child. She revealed the physical and psychological abuse she experienced at the hands of her family. We genuinely understood and sympathized with each other's pain.

I ended a fling I was having with a man and got back with Terry, a man I had dated off and on for four years. I loved him and was confused about my growing feelings for Renae. Eventually my housemate, Darcy, decided she wanted to move in with another friend. Renae found a higher-paying job and wanted a place of her own. Two new roommates moved in with me, and I tried to persuade myself that Renae and I should just be friends. I stayed busy going to school and working, but we talked on the phone every chance we got. My nights off were usually reserved for Renae. We shot pool, drank beer, and ate vegetarian food at the local restaurant.

On one unusually cold November night, I suggested that we skip the noisy bars, buy a bottle of wine, go back to her place, and build a fire. I wanted to see her new apartment, but I think we both knew what I had in mind, or at least what I hoped red wine and a cozy fire would lead to. When we reached her apartment, I was amused by the Zen-like emptiness. A desk, a mattress, a cat, and a free-roaming rabbit were all that occupied the interior of her rather spacious two-bedroom apartment. We built a fire and talked for hours. After finishing the red wine and listening to k.d. lang's *Ingenue* for the fifth time, Renae leaned against the wall. I yawned, feigning sleepiness and laid my head on her shoulder. Her smell was irresistible. I kissed the mole on her soft neck. Delicately, she kissed the inside of my palms, an erogenous zone I never knew existed. At last, after months of flirting, we were in each other's arms. I was finally kissing the soft, full lips I wrote about in my journal. Even today the taste of red wine and the music of k.d. lang remind me of that passionately charged first night with Renae.

Journal Entry: 11/16/92
Lazily feeling her body with my lips, I never tire of softness. What is it about Renae? We laugh together. She's so beautiful and funny. She told me she doesn't simply love me, she's very much in love with me. I'm so happy and alive lately.

I broke up with my boyfriend and practically moved in with Renae. I remember our first shower together and her bashful hesitancy. I remember showing her the poses I learned in yoga class in front of the fire in the nude. I remember our passionate good-bye kiss when she had to leave for work. We've been together for over four years now. As with any relationship there have been moments of passion and ecstasy as well as moments of boredom, wandering eyes, and jealousy. Through it all we have remained together because of our honesty, communication, and love for each other. I hope to know Renae for the rest of my life. I still feel the same intense passion for her now that I did when I wrote the following poem in my journal.

Journal Entry: 12/20/92
This woman becomes like a shroud—a balm for my eyes, my soul Slipping deeper into her, I feel the warmth my body craves I pour myself into her like water in a vessel—taking her shape upon me— I feel the contours—feel I know every rounded curve She changes form as quickly as the clouds—we become like air and breathe into each other—nourished and absorbed by the sun We wait to fall together like rain on the earth.

Sally Camper

BY GRETCHEN ZIMMERMAN

If you've ever been to the Michigan Womyn's Music Festival you would know what a completely different world it can be. It is also the last place I would ever expect to meet the boy-dyke, beefcake, dreamboat woman of my dreams, the woman I would want to share my life with.

Sarah and I met one bright sunny August morning under a yellow-and-white workers' tent at the festival. We had been assigned to the same work crew: security/communications. When I first laid my eyes on Sarah, she and a couple of crew members were performing a mock "This is my first time at the festival" demonstration for the rest of the crew. It was a funny skit, designed to show everyone on our crew what types of situations we would deal with as communication crew members. Sarah played Sally Camper, lost soul of the festival who had misplaced her tent, her girlfriend, and the direction of the front gate. Watching her amateur acting abilities, I thought she was an obnoxious, overly self-conscious, grunge leather dyke (no doubt from the West Coast), sporting a wallet chain and big, black, clunky boots. Later I would discover that she was a sincere, sweet, fashion-conscious, stylish grunge-looking leatherdyke from the Midwest. She had the personality to match.

What I did not know was that I would want to share my life with her. I did not know she was the beef-boat, dream-cake of my dreams until several nights later.

Our first conversation took place in the workers' tent after Sarah played ever-so-lost Sally Camper during midmorning break. The conversation was casual, small-talkish, and brief. I was talking to another security crew member, someone Sarah had known for years. Sarah joined us and began talking to her friend without acknowledging my presence, and I thought, *Well, how rude.* Nevertheless, I got excited when she said to her friend, "I brought my chess set this year, but I'll have to find someone to teach me how to play."

Now, I didn't know this comment was intended for me, and even to this day she claims it was. I fail to see how much about my overall boy-dyke demeanor screams: *I play chess!* And, furthermore: *I give lessons!*

So, of course, wanting to make new and fabulous festi-friends, and being overly thrilled at the prospect of knowing another leatherdyke who was interested in the fine art of playing chess, I said, "I'll teach you."

"You will?" she asked, pretending she suddenly noticed me sitting there next to her friend.

"Sure," I said, eager to get to know someone on the land.

And that was it. Our first conversation. It wasn't until a few days later that I talked to her again.

The next time we spoke was at our first overnight shift together, the dreaded midnight-to-8-in-the-morning shift. There were four of us at the gate that night, allowing two shifts if women went to sleep two at a time. Sarah and I found ourselves in the sleep-tent together for the first four-hour shift of sleep. We lay in the quiet, cold stillness of the tent and chatted for at least two out of the four hours. Then we decided it was best to get some sleep. I told her I really liked her a lot. She said her feet were cold and could we snuggle? Unlikely story.

"Sure," I said nonchalantly.

The next day I was in an unusually good mood. I ran into Sarah in the courtyard of the workers' common eating area and said, "Hey, I've got something for you."

She looked surprised. "What is it…?"

Before she could even get the full sentence out of her mouth, I kissed her long and hard. Being the butch dyke that she was, she was not used to other women, especially other boy-dykes, making the first move. But the ironic smile on her face told me that she didn't mind.

It wasn't until we played "pins and needles" a week later that my world turned upside down. She pierced me on my chest several times. Then, suddenly, I got severe menstrual cramps which unfortunately and prematurely ended the scene. She walked with me to the worker's health care tent and pampered me until I felt better. Never in my life had a woman been so nasty to me and so sweet all in the same night. I adored it. And her. We played again a few nights later (nonsexually), then the next day I caught a bus back across the country to Vancouver. That was when I knew she was the one for me.

What attracted me to Sarah the most—next to her pool-blue eyes and oh-so-scrumptious butt—was her sweet, gentle manner combined with her extremely tough, butch exterior. I've always loved boy-dykes, women who can pass as men when they want to, who get called "sir" on the streets and occasionally between the sheets, a butch-switch who is as tender as the day is long.

Although I did not immediately feel like I had known Sarah all my life, I did somehow know that I felt familiar with her. The only thing I can imagine its being like is driving past a really charming house that is not for sale so you never consider moving into it. It's not until the "For Sale" sign goes up that you consider living there. When you finally move in it feels like home, and you wonder why you didn't know it would feel that way every time you passed by it. Then you think, *Ah, yes, this is home. I've known it all along.*

During the two-day bus ride home from the festival I did nothing but think about Sarah. I kept wondering when I would stop thinking about her and start thinking about my lover back home. But I never stopped thinking about Sarah for a moment. I saw her face when I closed my eyes, heard her voice when I slept. My heart sank at the thought of never seeing her again.

At the time, Sarah lived in Seattle and I lived in Vancouver, Canada. The cities are only three hours apart, but it seemed like a million miles. But since I couldn't let this beautiful boy-dyke slip away from me, I took charge of the situation, left the woman I was living with, and moved to Seattle to be with Sarah.

It's been almost a year. The Michigan Womyn's Festival is fast approaching. I still haven't taught Sarah to play chess. We've been too busy. I think I'll teach her for her 80th birthday.

Who Needs a Glass Slipper When the Whole Ballroom's Transparent?

BY FAY JACOBS

Fifteen years later and we're still surprised we met at all.

With such opposite lives the fact that we wound up dancing together that March night in 1982 surely proves there is a thing called kismet.

I was 34 and recently sprung from the closet. My first lover was the original Mixed-Message Queen. She pursued me with an intensity that scared me right back into the closet before I finally fell head over heels for her. Then she felt suffocated. Go figure.

On one particular Friday night, she repeated her "You have to date other women" mantra so many times I wanted to barf. Instead I lied.

"It so happens I have a date tomorrow night," I said, smugly. Then I had to find something to do.

An acquaintance mercifully mentioned a women's dance in Baltimore at the Glass Pavilion on the campus of Johns Hopkins University. This being 1982, and me being right out of the wrapper, I had an attack of internalized homophobia. *What moron books a gay dance in a glass room? I'm not up for this*, I told myself.

That was just one of many things that compelled me to stay home that night. I was also navigationally challenged. I'd been in

D.C. for 16 years and still couldn't find Capitol Hill, much less Baltimore, without a tour guide. Moreover, it was unseasonably freezing outside.

"It's a good night to stay home and watch television," said my friend and housemate, Mary Jane. "I'm making mashed potatoes."

That was all I needed. I decided to stay home. Safe in my womb. Until Mixed-Message Queen called.

"What are you doing?" she asked.

Resisting the urge to say "Nothing, come on over," I mumbled, "I'm going out."

"If you insist," she replied. "I'll call you in the morning." I wanted to kill her.

With meat loaf and mashed potatoes cooking in the kitchen behind me, I bucked the odds and left.

Meanwhile, equally impressive barriers fell to send Bonnie out that same night. Free of a crappy relationship and happy to be on her own, she inexplicably accepted a casual date for the dance. But as the moment approached, she almost backed out. Her date, a horsewoman, was riding the hunt that afternoon, requiring Bonnie to meet her at Johns Hopkins. Did she really want to go? It could have swung either way.

The dance started at 9 o'clock, and I entered the nearly empty hall at one minute after. That was late for me, and I was a disheveled mess from riding my hunt to Baltimore. It was a glass ballroom, all right. I could see the lavender balloons from the street below.

Yearning for the mashed potatoes and the Mixed-Message Queen I had left behind, I consoled myself by listening to the all-woman New Age band tune up as women started arriving, mostly in pairs. A few shy-looking types hugged the room's perimeter, while others wandered in and clustered with friends. Finally I saw the couple who had gotten me into this.

"Hi," Amy waved.

"Glad to see you," I answered. Having no energy for games, I cut to the chase. "Know any available singles here?"

My friends exchanged glances and pointed to Bonnie across the room.

"I'm looking for someone who isn't screwed up," I cautioned.

Again they pointed to Bonnie. She was an attractive, nicely dressed woman desperately eyeing the door.

In a fit of completely uncharacteristic behavior, I marched over and introduced myself. I have no memory of the conversation, probably because the sounds of what I thought was the band tuning up turned out to be the actual music. It was deafening. So we got up to dance.

For two tortured minutes we tried to find the beat, our discomfort worsened by imagining a crowd outside watching us through the stupid glass walls. Finally I hollered over the music, "Let's go someplace where we can talk," and we fled toward our coats.

Just then, the horsewoman arrived. She was very imposing and had a set of teeth like the horse she had just dismounted. I started to sweat.

"We're just leaving," said Bonnie, slightly apologetically, but not altogether sorry.

To her credit, the mistress of the hunt shrugged and said, "I should have known better than to leave someone as good-looking as you here by herself."

Bonnie and I headed to a local women's bar. The wind sent twigs, leaves, and city trash swirling around Bonnie's car as we drove down St. Paul Street, past Baltimore Harbor, and into Little Italy. We hit every traffic light just as it turned yellow, with Bonnie hollering "Catch you next time!" as we sailed through. By the fifth amber light it was a duet.

The bar was as noisy as the dance, only we recognized the music. After our fill of "Bad Girls" and "Gloria," we retreated to the car and reversed directions. "Catch you next time!" we both shouted to the amber traffic lights.

Finally speaking below a scream, we talked and talked, discovering our differences. Bonnie was into softball and camping. I saw diamonds only at Bloomingdale's and never slept anyplace with turf between my bed and bath. My accent was Noo Yawk. Miss Baltimore said, "I love gewin' downy ocean, dewnt yew?" It took me ten minutes to figure out she meant a trip to the beach.

She owned a dental lab. I was dental-phobic. I directed plays. She had seen *Hello, Dolly!* once. She built things and wired whole buildings. I couldn't even stop my VCR clock from flashing.

We laughed as it got worse. I was obsessively early. She generally ran a little late. My Manhattan clan loved museums and contemporary furniture, and worked in advertising. Her people hailed from Virginia hill country, decorated Early American, and plowed for a living. She was DAR-eligible, and I was Ellis Island progeny. And there's no time to even mention religion.

Amid howling wind in a deserted parking lot, you could hear opposites attracting.

"My God! It's 3:30 A.M.!" I said, worrying about how early Ms. Push Me/Pull You would call.

"It's late. Stay at my place and go home in the morning," Bonnie offered.

"Um…I…Um…I really have to get home," I stammered. I sounded prudishly idiotic, or worse, not interested. I couldn't imagine reporting an all-nighter at morning debriefing.

"Really, you can sleep on the couch if you'd like," Bonnie tried.

"Um, sorry…I really have to be home…" I could just imagine what sort of lunatic she thought I was, because I was wondering too.

We exchanged phone numbers, promised to call, and I was back home for the 8 A.M. inquisition.

But Bonnie called the next day too. And before we knew it we were an item—sending my once-smothered girlfriend back into the thrill-of-the-chase mode.

It turned out that Bonnie and I were totally opposite in every way, except for our search for a grown-up, already through therapy and ready for a healthy relationship.

When it comes to the rest of the stuff, we are both proficient at compromise. I'm still directing shows, but now I bring along my own set builder. She traded camping for boating—it still involves ice coolers and bug spray, but there's carpet between the powerboat's berth and bath. We get everywhere exactly on time, rushing Bonnie and sending me into spasms about being late. She gets me to the dentist by telling me we're going shopping, then kidnapping me. I survive softball seasons in the bleachers—but I wear sneakers in case they need me, rather than forfeit for lack of players. It's never happened, so they don't know that using me would still be forfeiting. And every December we try not to burn down the Christmas tree with the Hanukkah candles.

Sure, occasionally we scream "Princess!" and "Hillbilly!" at each other, but it works out. And it turns out that my ex doesn't send mixed messages about friendship; she's great at it and supportive of us both. And just last week, Bonnie and I were on St. Paul Street, squeaking through a yellow light. "Catch ya later," we muttered.

We may be quieter than we were 15 years ago, but we're still opposites attracting.

Eternal Soul Mates

BY SHILPA MEHTA

The first time I saw her I knew she was the one. The lines that had been in my head for centuries sprang forth like the lava from a volcano, no longer able to control their captivity.

I have known you for lifetimes

Loved you for even more

Her eyes captivated me. I had to talk to her, find out her name. This was the moment I had been waiting for my entire life. As I took her hand in mine and gazed into those blue-green eyes, I knew my soul would no longer be lonely.

It was love at first sight for me. We met New Year's Day. In a crowded room full of lesbians ringing in the New Year at our local women's club, she was the most beautiful woman I had ever seen. When we first looked at each other it was as if, for a moment, time had stopped just for us. Her irresistible smile beckoned me to her side.

For the past year my love life had been what was affectionately described by friends as "power dating." I was single after another long-term relationship ended and was loving every minute of my dyke dating saga. Meeting Sara changed all that.

Suddenly the club that had become my second home started to feel claustrophobic. I went up to her and asked her to dance. She agreed. Waiting for a romantic song seemed like an eternity. As I fantasized about holding her close, feeling her arms around me, a sudden urge to be alone with her overtook me, and I asked her if we could go out for coffee instead. To my delight, she said yes.

She had already captured my soul with those captivating eyes; they were warm and inviting. When she spoke, her sexy voice further captured my heart. The final touch was her mind. Intelligent women turn me on. As we talked that evening, the conversation flowed naturally. There was an instant feeling of comfort and trust.

I did not want the evening to end because I was enchanted by this breathtaking, sexy, intelligent, tender woman I felt I had known forever. As we kissed good night my pulse was racing and my heart was pounding.

The only comfort I had in saying good-bye was knowing that we had made plans to see each other! Soon! I couldn't wait. I was breathless with anticipation, wanting it to be tomorrow already so that I could call her.

I went home, and all I could do was think of her. She called and left a message on my answering machine as promised. As I looked up and gazed at the stars in the sky, I remembered the twinkle in her eyes. The soft raindrops on my skin made me recall the caress of her fingers as we kissed. No other woman made me feel the way Sara did. It was at that moment that I knew I had found my soul mate. We were destined to be together.

Hey, Baby!

BY DREY H. FISHER

Aah...Pride Day! Less commercial than Christmas and more exciting than Thanksgiving, it is the day to break out the DYKES RULE T-shirt and create a loud, obnoxious (legal) ruckus with all your brothers and sisters in the middle of the street. It always leaves me buzzing with elation, even if it is plagued by rain or psychotic Christians telling us where to go.

This particular Pride Day took place on June 5, 1994, in my adopted hometown of Washington, D.C. I had plans to meet up with my best friend, Renee. Even though I was a 20-year-old college student and she was seven years my senior, we were two peas in a pod: handsome, single, broad-shouldered tomboys on an intrepid quest to catch the eyes (and hopefully more) of beautiful women everywhere we went. Therefore, our Pride Day plans included our usual brazen, yet trivial, flirting.

However, from the moment I awoke that day, plans were not materializing as usual. First of all, I was running late. If there is one thing that my father drilled into my head as a kid, it is that punctuality (even more than cleanliness) is next to godliness. So, rarely was I late for anything, especially something I was really looking forward to doing. During the five-block walk from my apartment to the Pride Festival site, my mind was churning on two main concerns: that Renee had left our planned meeting site and we would miss each other in the crowds, or that she had already met an ideal woman at the festival and I would be rendered a "third wheel," which I hate.

Upon my arrival I saw Renee sitting exactly where she was supposed to, casually talking to one of the most divine women I ever laid eyes on. I stopped a distance back so that I could observe for a moment those heavenly, luscious, chocolate-brown legs, smooth, curvy arms, and most copious lips. Rather than making any assumptions or falling into a fantasy, I quickly collected my thoughts and sauntered over to my beaming best friend and her newfound target of affection.

Renee immediately introduced me to Candice, and we greeted each other with a handshake and a brief moment of eye contact. Then Renee stated the fact that made all the difference in the world: that Candice, this ethereal female who defined sexy, was only 16 years old. An eleventh grader. Classic jail bait. My mind spewed out a quick justification that there was not that big a difference between 16 and 20, and I joyfully revealed my age in comparison with Renee's abundant maturity. It was at that moment my emotions began agitating and my mind started racing. Could this be the one? Or will her age get in the way? What if her parents were deranged homophobes wanting to send me to jail? But she was so exquisite, it was definitely worth the risk.

The three of us began strolling casually around the Pride Festival. Renee, good buddy that she was, walked ahead of Candice and me, leaving us alone to talk. I was my usual valiant self, asking lots of questions to stimulate conversation. I really wanted to know everything about her, but I couldn't tell if her giddiness was her true demeanor or if it was the excitement hiding a deep and complex personality. At that moment, I was so revved up I really didn't care which one it was. As we walked I noticed other things about her that I really liked: her soft, gentle hands; her hair in thick, shoulder-length braids; her big, darkest-brown eyes. Looking at her and walking close to her gave me a feeling of comfort combined with an edgy euphoria and rising libido. The feeling of risk and danger was present, considering that dating a 16-year-old would involve breaking of curfews, sneaking into clubs, and unauthorized sex. But, as the day progressed, a certain feeling of naturalness transcended all other emotions. Somehow I knew that if I were to delve into this, it would be real and serious and definite. There was no way that I could casually date a 16-year-old. If I was to be her introduction into dyke life then I was going to stick with her through the rest of it.

With that thought in mind, our day ended with me asking Candice to share a dinner date later that week. Upon her shy but affirmative reply, the rest, as they say, is history.

The epilogue is still unfolding. We successfully survived the trials and tribulations of teenage interracial lesbian love, and now embark on adulthood together. Needless to say, at ages 19 and 23, no one teases me about going to jail anymore, and her parents are not homophobic at all. We have been together for 2½ years and plan to move in together this summer.

Full Circle

BY FRANCI MCMAHON

Last night I asked her, "Did we meet at Nikki's making candles? Or was it in a cave?"

The details have faded after 32 years. No, we weren't together all of that time, but, perhaps, I should start at the beginning.

At the age of 23, my view of 16-year-old Jenifer was tolerant. I remember that she ran. Everywhere. Her brown hair was braided beyond her waist, and this long appendage flew straight behind her when she ran. Somehow, even while sitting, she appeared to be moving at high speed. Her smile was, is, enthusiastic and ready for whatever life dishes up. Good strong teeth, full lips in a wide mouth. Her eyes are the strange gray of two rocks striking together.

We lived in Washington, D.C. during the time of John Kennedy and the aftermath of his assassination. Queer roles were firm, waiting to be challenged and redefined. My friends and I fell somewhere between butch and femme. Most of the time I fancied myself butch.

Every weekend we headed for West Virginia to explore the wild limestone caves threading underground. We were all lesbians in the groups, but invariably, at least one man, knowing we were gay, would buddy up with us. My theory was that we were women without roles, unafraid to be daring, and this appealed to the sort of guy who hung out with us. Inevitably, though, our token male would find a girlfriend, and then they would both fade out of the picture.

The Washington, D.C., Spelunking Club bought an old frame house in the West Virginia mountains to use as a trip base. I didn't bunk there often, but friends of mine did. It was there I began hearing rumors about Jenifer, the "baby dyke."

At 16 she was "off-limits."

Among spelunkers she was known to go anywhere, push any lead. This reputation was awesome in a bunch who would exhale in a tight space in order to crawl forward, or slip off our overalls to slide between mud-covered rocks, dragging our carbide packs with the toe of one boot. Or we would wade neck-deep, carbide lights shining out over the water, through an underground stream to reach a high-vaulted cavern.

During the next couple of years Jenifer became a pester fly, hanging out with lesbians, wanting to know more about us.

Jenifer and I discovered that we had other interests in common.

She played the violin, as had my father. Our love of classical music bonded us deeply. So did our love of poetry. In her family home near the Washington Cathedral, we read out loud in the small basement room that held a well-worn couch. We brought poems as gifts. I read e.e. cummings, "All In Green Went My Love Riding," and many works by Edna St. Vincent Millay. I remember being near tears as I read to her of burning our candles at both ends and not lasting the night. Her deep voice read to me one of her favorites, the poem by Ralph Waldo Emerson, "To Each and All."

As she neared the legal line into adulthood, it was decided that I should tell her about our collective lesbianism. Her response was so dear: "Then I am too."

From then on this gal pursued me. And I her. We read poetry and kissed, and if her brothers or mother came down the noisy stairs we resumed reading. Flushed, I'm sure.

We had nowhere to go for lovemaking, and I was well aware of the implied threat of her father, the lawyer.

I shared an apartment with a caving buddy, a straight woman. Upon learning of my sexual preference she waged a vigorous campaign to warn off Jenifer. She also abruptly stopped sashaying through the apartment wearing only a towel on her head. That she knew I was queer was one thing, but I absolutely did not want my roommate to find me in bed with Jenifer.

Finally friends took pity on us and loaned us their house for an afternoon's worth of privacy. I was very tense. The whole situation began to feel more and more dangerous. I made love to her that day, but afterward I stopped calling her, became emotionally absent. It was my way of coping with a situation which appeared to beyond my ability to handle. *Run* was the word.

Jenifer wrote a strong and wonderful letter, but I never responded.

We saw each other occasionally, at parties or at a mutual friend's house. I heard through the grapevine that she became lovers with one of my ex-lovers. Then I heard she left for California.

Years and lovers passed. Years that I spent in Vermont. At times I was happy, but when I felt gloomy I'd dream about returning to my horse-filled, open-sky West. Eventually I reached the point of mailing out resumes to points west.

It was then I heard from an old friend that Jenifer was living in Montana, and had been for 20 years. She was doing what I wanted to do. Living my life. I wrote to her, thinking that when I moved there it would be great to have an old friend to hike and camp with.

I flew to Billings, Montana to travel the state, meet possible employers, and to actually see the Judith ranching area I had chosen as the setting for the book I was writing.

I first saw Jenifer again standing in front of her house, image superimposed in the rearview mirror of the rented car. We studied one another through the mirror. The moment felt significant, and I wanted to savor it. In so many ways she looked the same, though wrinkles made from character and sun graced her face. Gray had moused the brown of her hair. Her eyes were wary. Now we both carried the wisdom of experience and with it some damage to our innocence.

At dusk that evening we walked up into the dry, pine-covered mountains. In the high altitude and thin air we held hands as we walked. Friends.

We talked about loose ends. The letter she had sent me. Why I had emotionally left her. How she felt about me in her coming-out years.

The honesty put our past to rest so we could have a future. Electricity filled the air like a fast-moving summer storm. We took hold of the future which had waited so many years for us.

As I sit here writing this, I am looking out over the wide valley at the snow-covered mountains, Elkhorn and Crow. Coyotes sing as they come down from the mountains behind us. The horses wait along the fence for their hay; or, in the summer, they are dots far out in the yellow grass.

Two strong women, lovers, we have struggled in this relationship to keep our separate selves intact. Contentment seems an unfamiliar state to me, but I am growing more able to allow the peace to live within. My life has come full circle, to a place of love, strength, and warmth with an old friend, Jenifer.

Fat Dykes in Love

BY NANCY ASTARTE

Fat brought us together. In 1989 I was a member of Atlanta Fat Dykes, a support and activity group for lesbians over 200 pounds. In January of that year, our group decided to go to an exercise facility that was exclusively for heavy women. Because the place was in the suburbs and we were city dwellers, we decided to meet in a centrally located parking lot and ride together in one car: one very big car, an old wood-paneled station wagon, the only one that could hold us five women.

Though I was a big woman, I felt very confident, sensual, and beautiful that day. I dressed in a black- and white-striped leotard, thick black tights, and white aerobic shoes. Because I am such a femme, I wore a very tight belt to cinch my waist. I also pushed my breasts together to cause a six-inch cleavage to give the girls a thrill. It was a rare cold winter morning, so I covered up my femme fatale aerobic outfit with a long tweed coat.

When I got out of my car, I saw someone I didn't know standing with my friends. Holding a gym bag, she was dressed in only a red T-shirt and navy blue jogging pants. She was the type of lesbian who looked better in men's clothes than women's. I was attracted to her butchiness, so I approached the stranger with my hand extended and said in a cheery voice, "Hi! My name is Nancy." She shook my hand and said her name was Susan. When we got into my friend's station wagon, I sat in the middle of the backseat, so I would be between two women. Susan sat to my right, jammed up against me. I could feel her body shaking. "I can tell you're cold," I said. Wrapping my right arm around her shoulder, I pulled her even closer to me. We rode that way for the hour-long trip. I felt totally comfortable holding her.

When we arrived at the facility, we discovered that it was not a health spa with machines and other amenities, but only a room for aerobic exercise classes. As we joined the class, I chose the spot directly in front of Susan for my workout, and I threw myself into it. I wanted Susan to see that even though I weighed 215 pounds, I was in good shape and could keep up. It was fun showing off my flexibility for her, and I could tell she was watching what I was doing because I caught her staring at me several times.

As we were leaving, I gushed about the class, while Susan grumbled about it. She said she never would have come if she'd known it was only aerobics. She had brought her suit and expected a pool for swimming laps, her preferred exercise routine. She told me the only good thing about the class was watching me, especially seeing my thigh through the hole in my tights. She asked me if I had ripped my tights on purpose to show some skin. In shock, I slapped her arm and said, "No! Of course not!" I had split my seams—a fat girl's worse nightmare!

Mortified, I gradually recovered my dignity as our group walked next door to Ryan's Steak House for lunch, but I still gave Susan a hard time. When she told me she was getting her master's in English and wanted to be a professor, I asked her if she was going to be an "out professor" or a closeted one. She was taken aback by my question and said she didn't know. I could tell I had made her uncomfortable when I championed the importance of lesbian visibility. I think I was acting so aggressive because she had embarrassed me with that remark about the ripped tights. I wanted her to feel humiliated too.

I was over my pettiness by the time we left the restaurant. On the way home I sat up front, but turned around most of the way to face Susan. While we chatted I noticed that Susan was looking at me strangely, as if she had never seen anyone like me before. I took this to mean she wanted to get to know me better, but I had a long-distance girlfriend, which I had neglected to mention. I didn't want to lead Susan on or be disloyal to my girlfriend, so I first pulled out a photo of my dogs from my wallet to show to Susan, then a photo of me with my lover. She looked crestfallen as she held the photo and understood I was not single and available to date.

We met on a casual basis three more times during the next two weeks and slowly got to know each other. Discovering our common interests, we became friends—sharing meals, talking on the phone, visiting each other's houses, going to the grocery store together. Sometimes it's hard to tell if a lesbian is dating you or going out with you as a friend, but as the relationship deepened, we both felt the pulling on our hearts; we were falling in love.

One night after supper, I told her it was time, and she asked, "Time for what?"

"For us to make love," I replied. "It doesn't have to be now, or tomorrow, or this weekend, but soon."

Later that night we made passionate love fueled by weeks of pent-up desire. I confessed all this to my long-distance girlfriend, and she told me she didn't mind nonmonogamy. I did, as did Susan, so I broke up with the long-distance girlfriend. Susan moved in with me in April, and on June 16, 1989, we had our commitment ceremony in our home. We've been together ever since; and by the way, we're even fatter than when we first met.

Sleepless in China Rain

BY AMY FRANKLIN-WILLIS

Six years, a wedding, a transcontinental move, and our first "hello" escapes me. I do remember pegging you as a Pooh Bear at first sight. You were short, rounded in all the right places, and walked a Pooh Bear walk—kind of side-to-side, like a toddler.

I would see you strolling on the opposite side of the campus meadow. You would catch sight of me, raise your cinnamon eyebrows in surprise, and smile this slow, sweet smile, like I had just made your day. We'd greet with a hug. I'd sigh a silent *thank-you* to the heavens as you wrapped your arms around me.

I do remember the night in your dorm room. Three days before that I had summoned you to my room. I sat on the purple-sheeted bed facing you, finally pushed to the edge of the high dive that was my love for you. I jumped. You stood with your arms crossed over your chest and took it rather well, considering how you could have more easily expected me, your dear straight friend, to say I was an android from Jupiter. The feelings I had sheltered in a shimmering crystal box, only opening it when alone, were set free and neatly placed in your hands.

You invited me over to your dorm. There told me the stranger-than-fiction story of your growing up to test me, to see if I could handle all the truths you needed to tell. I sat on the hardwood floor across from you, my knees held tightly against my chest. You smelled of the China Rain you generously dabbed behind your ears, on your throat, and between and under your breasts. Sitting on a scratchy South American blanket I have since begged you to get rid of, you began hesitantly, shyly. Your voice gathered strength and speed as the mists of the past enfolded you. Rain danced lightly outside the half-opened window, coaxing the earth smells from the ground and bathing the campus anew. Your child's tale wove itself around me, swirling all of your mysteries into place like a quiet tornado. When you finished with a "Well, that's it," your Parrish-blue eyes locked with mine. Sensing safe harbor, our souls reached across the distance to embrace for a moment and rest within one another.

At 1 in the morning, we went for a walk, arm in arm, touching this way for the first time. The grandfatherly eucalyptus trees bent shelter toward us as we followed the clouded shadow of the moon. We laughed at the din of the pond's ribbiting frogs. Warm rain fell upon us like a blessing.

When we neared El Campanile, you stopped and turned to face me. You loved the Campanile, you said. The look on your face was one I did not recognize, and it made me nervous. You smiled that "I want to kiss you smile" I now respond to as surely as the sound of my name. I stared down at our interlocked hands—your smaller and sturdier one fit neatly into my more fragile-looking hand. We walked on.

I returned to your room. I wanted to stay, to wrap my arms around you and sleep in the warmth of your skin, which always smells as if you've just come in from the sun. I needed you to ask me to stay. You didn't. Instead we hugged, and I went home alone.

I slept little.

Subsequent to a Brief Delay

BY SHELLEY RAFFERTY

We Raffertys are a boisterous lot. We get drunk at funerals, play cards after Thanksgiving dinner, watch too much television, and drive a little recklessly. I grew up in a household that had far too much traffic—neighbor-kids and cousins, delivery and repair people, boarders from the local minor league baseball team, and a steady stream of my mother's boyfriends.

My dad left when I was nine, a departure that was eclipsed by a rapid succession of residences and a sudden immersion into the world of food stamps and AFDC. In addition to his middle-class income, Dad also took his college education with him, as well as the leather-bound books and intelligent discourse, the stern capacity for debate and problem-solving, and dreams of a life that included a two-car garage.

By the time I made it to high school I was torn between a distant memory that promised me a career in law or international relations, and the sobering reality of growing up in rental housing, second-hand clothes, and the necessity of going to work at 15.

I have no idea what sent me to German class.

But I know what kept me there.

Mandy sat in the second row from the door in the second seat from the front. I sat behind her, to her right, where I couldn't help noticing her chestnut-and-auburn hair, which fell to the middle of her back. She was a studious sort. Each day found her in class before me, her head bent seriously over a silly textbook, her voice reluctant when called upon, but her response always correct.

It seemed to me that she always carried too many books. I often wondered what classes she could be taking that required her to read the French *philosophes,* and such a wide variety of 18th- and 19th-century novels. *Wuthering Heights* was her favorite.

It took several weeks before we spoke to one another. Although I didn't consider myself easily intimidated, Mandy was a year older than I, shy yet clearly intelligent, and beautiful. She usually wore skirts and dresses to school. I wore jeans.

Maybe because I'm gabby, I got her attention. I played a lot of Scrabble with an elderly lady who lived across the street from me (her son was a producer of *The Munsters*—a Hollywood connection that thrilled me), so my vocabulary was large and pretentious. I guess Mandy liked that. I think she liked a lot of things about me, even though years later I came to understand that she liked how she felt about herself when she was with me even more.

In October she asked me to be on her Model United Nations debate team. We got to be the United Kingdom. I was a good arguer, and I set about my task of preparing for the debate with vigor.

At night we discussed our strategy on the phone.

I think we knew (although we didn't voice it) that something about our attraction for each other required a certain secrecy; as a consequence our German, combined with an improvised English shorthand that only we understood, improved rapidly.

I wrote poetry. We contrived ways to see one another after school. We wrote letters (which now number in the thousands), talked about literature, politics, poetry. Anything but boys.

That was funny, because we both had occasional boyfriends, although she had more than I. I was drawn to good Catholic faggots for reasons I could not figure out. Mandy, away from the eyes of her stern Presbyterian parents, indulged the boys with a wilder side. For a long time I knew nothing of these boys, and that was good. My jealousy and possessiveness, which she echoed, burned in me like a dormant virus. I tried to ignore it.

In December we went to Boston for a debate. Our shared hotel room offered us our first glimpse of our sexuality and our isolation. Our time together was strangely charged. We skipped most of the competition, ventured out to Harvard, to the subway, to the colonial streets in an ice storm. We returned to the quiet room laughing and frozen.

Mandy could not shake the cold.

I went to get something to eat. When I returned the bathroom door was slightly ajar, and I pushed it open to see if Mandy was all right. The room was steamy with condensation from hot bathwater. I had never seen her naked, and I was dumbstruck. I felt the heat rise to my face—not from embarrassment, but from recognizing something in myself, a flush of wanting her. We stared silently at one another, both knowing, yet not knowing, that something had changed.

We were too young, too shy, and too ignorant to act on our feelings. We didn't interact sexually, but we held hands, hugged often, shared cigarettes in study hall, took long walks, and tried to imagine life without each other. Early on, we knew we didn't want to be apart.

And then: graduation. We didn't know other women like us, and our parents disapproved of our attachment. Ultimately we shipped off to different colleges and relationships, although we kept the letters up and buried our longing for each other deep inside for nine years.

In 1980 Mandy came to get me. I forgot everything I knew and didn't know and fell into bed with her. It was if we had always slept together, as if we always would.

Eighteen years later we are still together. She is my anchor, my promise, my muse and friend...my colleague, fellow traveler, and adventurer...my hope and lover. She is all of my past that is worth salvaging, and all of my tomorrows.

It has not been an easy journey. There have been other lovers for both of us. And children. Four girls for her and a boy for me. We have survived poverty, flight, separation, violence, indifference, anger, jealousy, and abandonment.

But we have also shared poetry and joy, tenderness and loss, generosity and storytelling, passion, dreams, and desire. We know each other well and yet keep secrets still. From time to time we indulge the sweet regret of not becoming lovers in high school, but we are products of our time.

Luckily we are still young, and the road ahead is long.

We don't know if we can stay together. In some ways we are inseparable, committed by the permission that first allowed us to be and love ourselves, and our devotion to one another. But this permission is also a kind of bondage. Because it was forged from the fiber and ore of adolescence and identity formation, it has been difficult to allow one another to change and grow and become something "other."

For no, we are sharing the will to look ahead, to take some risks, and to let go of each other a little. It isn't easy. But we love one another enough to recognize that change is the only thing we can count on.

We are both changing.

And we are still together.

We remain hopelessly in love with one another.

Flaming Fag Hag

BY S.J. BLIGHT

I had been dating a woman who, I have since come to realize, was probably diagnosable as having Borderline Personality Disorder. Every time she made my life hell, I wrote it down in my calendar and highlighted it in yellow. At the end of one three-month period, I counted 104 highlights. One hundred and four times in 92 days was a pretty bad average. I knew that our limbo-love was not meant to last.

She had a best friend of 20 years named Alicia. I first met Alicia at my girlfriend's house. She was straight and had a boyfriend. I liked her right off and felt comfortable with her, even though I usually feel shy and awkward meeting new women. She seemed kind and maternal and, in fact, had two children who were nearly grown. She worked full-time as a counselor and part-time as a massage therapist. We had an old friend in common, a gay man. Alicia was a little in love with him. It occurred to me that she was a fag hag, and her looks fit the stereotype.

Alicia is a tall, full-figured, buxom woman with beautiful features, large reddish-brown eyes, full lips, ample makeup, and big, medium-length, curly red hair. She is of Portuguese descent. She dressed femme-funky style. When I first met her, I didn't dwell on the buxom or beautiful part. She was, after all, my girlfriend's best friend. She was also straight and living with a boyfriend. But I did notice that she exuded something—to this day I'm not quite sure what. She flames—her hair, her features, her voice, her personality, her temper, her love and her love of life. She's exuberant and funny. I assessed when I first met her that she was a flaming fag hag. And I liked her a lot.

As time went on I saw Alicia occasionally. I felt drawn to her, but not sexually. I liked her as a friend, but there was something more. I liked thinking about her being out there in the world. She made me feel connected, and she made life and my hometown seem more colorful.

I finally broke up with my girlfriend and spent a year single. Toward the end of that year, I started running into Alicia around town—at an Italian food store with her boyfriend, at a concert alone. After the concert we had an impromptu dinner together at a nearby lesbian restaurant. I hadn't really talked to her for over a year. It turned out she had ended her friendship with my old girlfriend. As we were winding up dinner, she asked me to do some handywoman work for her and promised me dinner and a massage in return. I readily agreed.

Looking back, I think I kind of on-purpose wore my strap-on tool belt to her house that August day. I was quick and efficient. Her boyfriend followed me around and was neurotic. The three of us were in the basement and, referring to me, Alicia exclaimed, "I feel like S.J. is part of the family!"

The dinner was delicious. She served it proudly, seating only me at the head of the table. Later she gave me an amazing massage, a flowing thing, the likes of which I had never experienced. During the massage, we talked. I told her about my job. She rubbed my shoulders and breathed, "That sounds like hard work."

There was a long pause. "Do you do many massages, now that you're a counselor?" I asked.

"Only like this...when it's fun." There was another long pause. She was wearing short shorts and a dark brown tank top, low-cut, that showed her cleavage.

Later, as we sat at her kitchen table, with her boyfriend wandering around the kitchen, the three of us talking, I caught something colorful in my peripheral vision. I turned my head to the left and focused, realizing then what had caught my eye. The little pink ribbon on the front of Alicia's tank top, right at the hollow between her breasts. She caught me staring and looked me straight in the eye. I quickly looked away.

I walked on air for the rest of the week. Later I told my therapist that I fell in love with Alicia that day. I remember telling her there was no one I'd rather spend time with than Alicia.

We started seeing each other on Friday nights, her free night away from her boyfriend and children. Those dates became very important to me. Alicia dropped hints like, "I've been told that once you get with a woman, you'll never go back to men."

I totally ignored these hints since I considered her to be straight and in a relationship, but gradually things developed and on one fateful Friday night we shared our first kiss. All I remember thinking was, "Uh-oh."

Big life arrangements and some pain had to follow for us to be together. Some people think our story is a little seedy, soap opera-ish at best, but we've been together for nearly two years. Although it's a little fiery at times, it feels right, and we want it to last, and—on some level—we know it's our destiny.

Breaking the Cold

$\int$he was electric. The acoustic guitar slung low across her hips wasn't plugged in and the microphone pressed close to her mouth was barely on, but she didn't need anything more. Her voice wasn't silk, it was steel, barely containing a rough darkness that transfixed me. Her hands, incredibly smooth and long against the black skin of her guitar, drew something from inside my coldness, bringing hot blood to my face. The room, usually too chilly, now was warm enough to bring damp sweat to my neck, making my collar rub painfully.

I was the music manager at a little bar I had worked in for far too long. Usually on Thursdays I was stuck behind the counter, pouring drinks for ungrateful students, but this evening at least, I had lucked out. That it was a shitty job and the hours were too long and too late didn't matter to me. There was nothing to go home to anyway. I had stopped caring.

But now I was caught halfway between the bar and the sound booth, not sure why I couldn't turn away from this woman standing alone onstage. She was beautiful, yes, with her soft, true-gold hair brushing her shoulders, her blue eyes half closed against the stage lights. She was hardly the first, though. A dozen beautiful women musicians had passed through these doors in the last year. None of them had ever gotten more than a handshake and a paycheck from me.

This was something else, something that caused everything but her voice and quiet strumming of her guitar to disappear. I finally managed to make it to the booth. I stood there for a moment, tugging slowly on the sleeve of the sound guy, who also happened to be my best friend. Harlan turned to me, making another tiny adjustment to the board before smoothing back his sandy hair. His smile was radiant, as always, when he saw me. He was and always will be the only man I really give more than a damn about. The harsh scraping of a chair made me wince as he dragged over a seat for me.

"What's up, chief?"

He must have asked me the question twice before I remembered what I was doing and stopped staring at the singer now starting her third song. The music was shadowed and powerful, making it difficult for me to concentrate.

"What was her name again?" I asked.

He leaned toward me, glancing at the subject of my interest. "McDavid is the last name. I don't remember the first. She's pretty good. Do you like her stuff so far?"

I nodded, pulling my chair closer to the rail of the booth, laying my head on my arms as the song closed over me. If Harlan said anything else, I didn't notice. Everything was forgotten; nothing except the smoke and heat of the singer's voice, nothing besides those smooth, perfect hands mattered. Her throat moving against the silver of her shirt was enthralling. I hardly noticed when she reached the end of her set. The time seemed far too short.

"Hey, Laura, are you going to pay the nice girl?" Harlan's voice broke through to me, sending me tripping upward off the bar stool. The coldness and the fear pushed back into the spaces the music had soothed into silence. I had to get out of there before the ice consumed me completely.

"Yeah, I'll get it, then I really have to leave. Would you tell the girl that I will be right back with her check?"

He nodded, giving me a strange, sad look that I ignored. I rushed to the office, running over several people in the process, to get the singer's money so I could go home. When I returned, a brief, strange panic overcame me. I couldn't find her. Standing on my toes between three frat boys who were rank with beer and cigarettes, I nearly yelled when someone laid a light touch on my shoulder.

Her speaking voice was no less devastating than her song. It was low, but not rasping, with a slight lilt at the end of each word, as flawless and beautiful as her hands. Something that still shakes me even now.

"Are you looking for me?" she quietly asked.

Tiny creases at the edge of her lips bent upward as she looked down at my hand, closed tightly around her night's wages. All thoughts of running from the bar disappeared, suddenly everything turned around. I was afraid to give her the money, afraid she might leave before I got a chance to figure out what was happening to me. She was only inches taller than I, but the distance seemed like years. The worn blue of her eyes held long spaces I was frightened to cross.

She took the envelope, brushing her fingers against my wrist. I didn't mean to, but I closed my eyes, unable to do anything more, unwilling to risk trying.

"I saw you over in the sound booth." Her words sounded like music. "Harlan said you were leaving. Would you mind staying a little longer?"

Her name was Elizabeth.

With Every Beat of My Heart

BY JULIA WILLIS

"*C*an you feel it?" Claire shouted into the microphone. The crowd of women responded with a roar of screams and applause. Oh, yeah. They could feel it, all right.

Claire was the lead singer in a women's rock group called The Ina Ray Band. One late October night 17 years ago they were headlining at The Paradise in Boston. I was there because a few weeks earlier I had moved into a house where Claire and the band rehearsed. I'd only briefly met Claire and the other women who lived there because I'd been in New York working with a comedy troupe. I hadn't even unpacked, and I had a miserable cold, but it was a great opportunity to see the band play and spend an evening with the people I lived with. So far I'd only heard them through the heating vents. I couldn't resist.

The club was packed with rabid fans, but my roommates saved me a seat at a table overlooking the dance floor. When Ina Ray took the stage the place went wild. This was more than just another headlining act. These were rock-and-roll women kicking ass, and it was love.

When people debate the question of love at first sight, there's always a question in my mind of what that phrase means to them. Is it a raging hormonal impulse or a spiritual epiphany? Or is it, as

Rock Hudson said to Doris Day in *Pillow Talk*, "just like a potbellied stove on a frosty morning?" And if we aren't sure which of these it is, how are we to know when it comes along?

The Ina Ray Band. Six women in red-and-black stage clothes doing an eclectic mix of funky rock and roll and synthesizer novelty tunes. They were an interesting cross between a Vegas lounge act and early techno-punk.

I especially took note of their drummer, first because she was so good, but also because she was not at all what I was expecting. Around the kitchen table at home, I had heard someone talking about the drummer. They referred to her as Moose. Immediately I pictured a big girl with powerful arms and thighs, wailing away unmercifully on a cheesy little drum kit. Instead, an elfin woman who couldn't have weighed 90 pounds soaking wet came on stage and ducked behind a huge blue-satin flame set of Slingerland drums with four crash cymbals and half a dozen concert toms in a configuration she learned from Karen Carpenter (of course, that was before A&M Records took Karen off the drums, stuck her in a dress, and told her to lose some weight). On those drums she played some of the best beats and most tasteful fills I'd ever heard from a drummer, *any* drummer. It was an extraordinary combination of power tempered with restraint; an exhibition in refined drumming; Keith Moon if he only knew when to quit. In other words, a very talented dyke.

While she was obviously the best musician in the bunch, the band's groupies were screaming for the players who weren't hidden behind their instruments. They screamed for the flashy lead singer in her fuck-me pumps, for the guitar player doing her best Mick Jagger scowl, the terminally cool blond on keyboards, the cute butch on bass who plucked hard and grinned sideways, even for the mugging sax player who was always a beat behind. Strange what impresses people, what turns them on. Being a performer myself, to me all that up-front attitude was just so much stage bullshit. Fun, but nothing to get excited about. Ah, but that nearly invisible magician holding the music together…now she was intriguing. The perfection in her drumming…that was impressive.

I often wonder if the reason people become disillusioned about love is because whatever it is that happens to them at first sight, plunging them headlong into one disastrous affair of the heart after another, isn't love to begin with, but a superficial infatuation that passes for love, a false quickening of the blood based on looks or moves or memory. Just another fleeting affection to be traded in on a newer model once the fresh leatherette smell is gone. And I wonder if real love can be listened for as well as seen, with one ear to the ground anticipating its approach.

I never intended to find love that night. My only plans were to catch the band, pick up a roast beef sandwich at Riley's on the corner and a half-pint of coffee brandy at Blanchard's across the street, then go home to nurse my cold and unpack my thermal underwear. Instead I ended up at a party in a fourth-floor walk-up in the South End's Bay Village. It was an Ina Ray after-gig party hosted by Claire's girlfriend. Michelle, one of my new roommates, talked me into going. "Come on, I promise we'll only stay an hour," she said. "You'll still get home early and you can unpack tomorrow."

So there I was at 1 in the morning, sitting by a window overlooking the Mass Turnpike, talking to a big black comic named Jimmy Smith about the comedy scene in Los Angeles.

"Ah, it's bad out there," he said. "Not like here. You got comics heckling each other, doing all kinds of nasty shit, real dog-eat-dog."

Just as he was really bumming me out, a young woman bounced right over to us and hopped into his lap, disrupting our serious conversation and being a perfect little pest. But neither of us minded. She did it with such grace, such innocence, like something a child would do. We were the comics, but she made us laugh.

I have no recollection of what she said in those first few moments after she arrived. I was too busy looking at her eyes. I had never met anyone with eyes so clear, so guileless. It was shocking, really. There was something about her that was not of this earth. She seemed to belong somewhere much kinder. I think my mind was so busy trying to assess what planet she might have come from that it took me a while to realize she and Jimmy were talking about the show. Then it clicked. She was Ina Ray's drummer. She was Laurel. The Moose.

Speaking as one whose cynical frame of mind was nurtured since birth and has left my more romantic friends shaking their heads in despair, I can verify there really is such a thing as love at first sight. Or, in my case, love at first sound. I know it's easy to be distracted by cheekbones, or lust after cleavage, or find beauty in a thigh line, but to hear a person's soul reverberating across a dozen drumheads is magic. To then have that magic verified in the gentle alien eyes of a woman who was clearly sent to love and be loved by you, now that's real luck. It might even be destiny.

I don't remember at what point Jimmy left us. I do remember Laurel telling me she got the nickname, Moose, because the band teased her for taking wildlife pictures on a road trip. I remember looking around and thinking we were the only people in the room laughing, that everybody else seemed bored or pissed off. I know I was drinking vodka and grapefruit juice, and when Laurel went to make me another she came back with an awful concoction of rum and grapefruit because they were out of vodka. I poured it into an elephant-ears planter when she wasn't looking. When Michelle asked me if I was ready to go, Laurel quickly offered to give me a ride later, and I accepted.

I remember us dancing to Aretha singing "Rock Steady," and how silly Laurel was, yelling, "Aretha!" whenever she spun around. I remember shortly after that Claire and her girlfriend had a fight about the volume of the music and several of us were recruited to remove Claire's stereo system and carry it down three flights of stairs to the street. We loaded it into Laurel's 1973 Dodge Dart, then Laurel drove Claire and me home. Not much of a party, really, except for the fact I met Laurel there. Seventeen lovely years ago. And still the beat goes on…

The Afternoon Girl

BY BRENDA S. SKINNER

When I met my long-term partner I was 32 years old and engaged to the man I'd been living with since college.

I had been working in a small law firm for several years. There was a series of college-age women working there for a semester or two. They were called the "afternoon girls." They answered the telephone in the late afternoon when the regular receptionist went home. I found them to be more interesting to talk with than the other women at work, whose lives seemed as boring as mine had become. With the "afternoon girls," I found myself reliving my college years and wondered what had happened to that part of me—the activist, the pot-smoker, the daring person who now was quite domesticated, whose best friend was her fiancé, Clyde. I talked about him constantly. I had no else to talk about.

I came back from lunch that summer day to find our cheerful Italian receptionist, Tina, talking to the newest afternoon girl.

"Hi, Miss Brenda. This is MaryKay." Tina called everybody "Miss." I looked MaryKay over. She had very short, boyish blond hair, no makeup, and was wearing blue Gap trousers. She appeared rather low-key. "MaryKay cut off all her hair yesterday," said Tina.

Again I looked at MaryKay. I didn't remember her coming past my desk for her interview. I could not picture her with long hair, and the short hair reminded me of the straitlaced religious kids I'd gone to college with.

"Miss Brenda lost 30 pounds." Tina was still talking.

This time MaryKay looked me over, then asked, "Oh? How?" Her voice was calm and pleasant.

"Weight Watchers." I was a big fan of Weight Watchers at the time. I began to talk about what they had done for me.

"Can you watch the front desk while I show MaryKay around?" Tina asked.

"Sure." I set down my bag and picked up *Time* magazine.

I turned to watch them walk away. MaryKay was built like some of the women I admired in college—low to the ground, sturdy, nice round hips. And she was wearing pants on her first day at our conservative law firm. I was mystified.

She buzzed me a few times that first afternoon with procedural questions. One of her responsibilities was dropping off the mail. At the end of the day she asked me what she should do if there was more mail to carry than she could handle. I told her to leave it for me. When I looked in the bin, I found one thin airmail envelope. I wondered why she couldn't handle it, telling my boss with a laugh that the new afternoon girl was a bit strange.

She quickly got under my skin. She had a cool, deadpan way about her that I could not stand. I am a Leo—passionate, quick to anger. She could be quite offhand, relaxed.

I got particularly irritated about her live-in boyfriend who called often. MaryKay and I would be in the middle of a fascinating political or feminist discussion when he would call, and she would talk to him as if I wasn't even there. One Friday, before a long weekend, MaryKay asked me to type her nursing school application essay for her. After I finished she took the application and left early to go to a movie with her boyfriend. I didn't understand why I felt so upset the rest of the day.

MaryKay often read *Ms.* magazine and even the queer Chicago papers at the front desk. I nicknamed her the "the feminist." She offered me her Ms., and I hid it in my desk drawer to read later. We had lengthy discussions, and I found myself staying well past closing time to talk to her. Despite my occasional irritations, I felt able to talk freely with her about anything—my secret curiosity about trying heroin, my questioning of my missionary parents' Christianity, the fact that Clyde had frequently told me that some day I would leave him for another woman. (We exchanged a long look over that remark.) One day as we talked she leaned back to stretch, giving me a glimpse of her smooth white belly. I thought to myself, "Hmm…nice."

One afternoon I handed her a favorite story I had written called "Sara." It was about a woman who falls in love with her female roommate. Ironically, I wrote it within the first two months of moving in with Clyde. I loved the story. I sat at my desk as she read it, nervously waiting for her to buzz me and tell me what she thought. The buzz did not come. Casually, I walked past the front desk. She looked up at me with the most pleased smile on her face and continued to read in silence. After office hours, she stopped by my desk and said simply, "It's magnificent."

A week later she gave me some of her own poems, one of which was about being in love with her best female friend in college. I loved thinking of MaryKay that way and found myself wishing the poem was about me.

On a rainy Friday night in February, she walked me to Clyde's office. It was Valentine's Day. Sheltered under a umbrella we talked freely, as always. I was upset with someone's pettiness at work and even more annoyed with myself for getting caught up in it. I told her how different I used to be, how in college I had been an activist for gay rights.

"Have you had any experience with women?" she asked.

"One. But we agreed never to talk about it. How about you?"

"Yes. Sometime I'll get drunk and tell you about it." She was quiet for a moment. "Actually I left three men because I wanted to make love to a woman."

After leaving me at Clyde's office, she went to her parents' suburban home for the weekend. I sat with Clyde and his friends, drinking beer after beer, exhilarated, unable to stop thinking about her. At four in the morning, drunk, headachy, and giddy, I sneaked out of bed and began writing about her in my journal. The next day I dropped a sealed note off to her, care of her boyfriend.

Come Monday we were both excited and nervous to see one another. She had read my note and written one of her own, ending with a quote from *Casablanca:* "This looks like the beginning of a beautiful friendship."

She offered me a ride home from work that night, the first of many. We began to look forward to our daily time alone together. No one at work suspected anything. We had impassioned conversations in that small car of hers. I barely ate or slept and was unable to keep quiet about her to Clyde.

A week after that walk in the rain, MaryKay found me in our secluded file room. She handed me a poem she had written:

> RAIN
> yes, I am okay
> (you asked as you were stepping out of the car)
> I seem distracted, I know.
> it's just that
> I have been drawn in
> by your beautiful brown eyes
> your tender listening deep eyes
> gently nodding your head
> to tell me that

a connection is being made
and getting deeper
don't be afraid, please.
I will be tender where it may hurt
and everywhere else.
cup your hands
I find I am pouring my heart
like water.

We then drove to her Catholic alma mater, where we strolled along the beautiful lake in the early evening. I shyly took her hand. We stopped in front of a small chapel in the soft shadows where she reached up to me for our first kiss. I could see the white waves dancing like dolphins under the full moon over her shoulder.

Our lives were forever changed in that moment.

Straight and Safe

BY S.R. KINGLY

I first noticed Tina at Sisterspace & Books, an African-American women's bookstore in D.C. I noticed her out of the hoard because of her bold, short haircut. I am attracted to women with short hair. The more severe the cut, the more attracted I am. Next I examine the facial features, and last the shape of the body. This is my usual procedure for admiring women I find attractive.

Tina was almost bald. She had a beautiful face, with playful, smiling eyes, a succulent mouth, and a small, well-built frame with ample breasts and bottom. Physically she more than passed my muster. To say she is beautiful is an understatement. She was and is "drop-dead" gorgeous. Since gay and straight women frequented the bookstore, I assumed she was straight, but there was something about her…

I left it alone. Since I was in a long-term, long-distance relationship when I met Tina, I acknowledged that I found her attractive and filed it away. I wasn't looking for a lover, but I needed a friend.

I attended workshops and book signings at the store for about a month and only saw Tina there on a casual basis. Occasionally we shared ideas and feelings about relationships, computers, books. Nothing too deep, nothing too revealing. From our few short interactions I was convinced she was straight and, therefore, safe for me to confide in and perhaps cultivate a friendship with. I didn't trust

myself to confide in a fellow lesbian if I was attracted to her. I was
in a vulnerable state. My best friend had died of AIDS a few months
prior, and I was unable to share my pain and feelings with my lover.
I was never good at revealing my true self to anyone I was romantically involved with.

One fateful Friday I was in a particularly needy state. My absen-
tee lover was not scheduled for a visit that weekend, and I needed
her. I called her to see if we could meet even briefly. She didn't
think it was a good idea, but I vacillated between surprising her anyway and waiting for the needy feelings to subside. In the meantime
I had dinner and went to the bookstore for a reading and book sign-
ing by a local author. Tina was there.

After the event the owner of the store asked Tina to give me a ride
home. I went flush. Tina reluctantly acquiesced. My reaction surprised
me. I felt excitement and danger as we gathered our coats in silence
and headed for the door. On the sidewalk outside I asked Tina to join
me for a nightcap. I wasn't sure how she would respond. She accepted. We went to the restaurant down the street where I had dined earlier. Tina's warm and nonjudgmental attitude made it easy for me to
open up to her. I told her about my relationship, and she didn't run
away. We talked like old friends. I was open and honest with her and
the hours flew by. We talked until 2 in the morning. It was snowing
when we left the restaurant, and she drove me home as promised. I invited her to sleep on the sofa because driving was treacherous. De-
clining my offer, she drove home in the blinding snowstorm.

The following day she called and invited me to a movie. I accepted. My lover warned me that I was heading in a dangerous direction.
I didn't listen. I wanted to see Tina again. I admitted that I had feelings for her, but I convinced myself that I was safe. Tina was straight.

In a letter Tina confessed that she was attracted to me. Being the
seasoned dyke, I tried to convince her that it was only an infatuation

and it would pass. Although her presence stirred passionate feelings within me, I was not looking for a fling with an enamored virgin chick. My days of turning out curious straight women were over. Tina told me she had had an intense and pleasurable relationship with a woman before and that she wanted a woman lover again. She wanted me. I was speechless. Here was this absolutely beautiful woman, and I mean beautiful inside and out, who desired me, thought I was beautiful, and told me so again and again. I thought I was dreaming, or worse—being the skeptic that I am—that someone was playing a prank on me. That was not the case.

Tina was relentless in her pursuit. I found her attention emotionally soothing, her presence physically and spiritually exhilarating. Tina's spirited yet mysterious eyes enticed me to come and play even as they warned me to stay away. Her full lips were seemingly molded into a perpetual pout which I found extremely sexy. I imagined what it would be like to press my lips against them. I got moist just thinking about it. I wanted her too. But my conscience was not clear because of the relationship I was in. I had never desired to cheat on a lover before. Not until I met Tina.

After some vacillation on my part, I took Tina to my bed. When we came up for air three days later, I knew she was the *one* for me. Over this period of time we laughed, we cried, we talked about all sorts of things. I admired her strength, her vulnerability, her sensitivity, and her wisdom. She has a playful little girl in her that touched and released the little girl in me. We bonded on a level much deeper than I had ever achieved before with another human being.

I ended the long-distance relationship. Tina and I maintained our separate apartments and got to know one another for a year before we moved in together. We celebrated our two-year anniversary in February. Our love and friendship are still strong.

Potluck Passion

BY LAURA HAMILTON

Heading to my first lesbian potluck, I suddenly developed a raging bad mood. It had been a warm, golden Saturday when I woke up, and my confidence had been brimful. I'd put off attending the monthly lesbian event, waiting for some magical right time. With the hint of spring in the air, I found new courage that morning.

A friendly-sounding woman answered the telephone when I called to ask for directions to the potluck. She said that night would be a great time to come because it was her first time hosting the potluck and there would be a lot of new women there.

By early evening, however, the promises of spring vanished, and wintry clouds began to weep. My mood followed the drop in temperature. I began to question what I was doing. I scathingly told myself there was no use in trying to meet someone by going to the home of total strangers. I was bound to be disappointed, an inner voice counseled. And wouldn't it be more comfortable just to rent a video and spend a familiar, safe evening with my three cats?

Despite my misgivings, shortly after sunset I found myself at the grocery store, pondering over the proper thing to bring to the potluck…I mean, if one were going to go. I wandered the aisles feeling worse and worse. Nothing seemed appropriate; everything was either full of preservatives, needed heating, or was simply unappetizing. I finally chose a few pippin apples and headed to the dairy section. I stood for a few minutes, overwhelmed by the array of cheese, but I eventually left the store with a block of Colby and a package of Gruyere in addition to the apples. At least I would enjoy what I brought, I thought.

On the pretext of "just driving by," I discovered the house was surrounded by cars. As I fought to parallel park in a too-small space, I wondered if anyone was standing at the window watching this fool move back and forth a dozen times. I sat in my car, willing my sweat to dry, feeling overwhelmed by the prospect of walking into a house filled with strangers. Any thought of having fun had vanished. I was merely determined not to let this challenge get the best of me.

Grimly I grabbed my pathetic paper sack and walked across the wet grass and up the front steps. No doorbell was visible, and judging by the volume of laughter and music penetrating the walls, it would have been useless anyway. Edging the front door open, I stopped. The crowd inside was wall-to-wall. I slithered into the house and wormed my way between bodies in search of the kitchen.

Fortunately the kitchen was slightly less crowded, and I found a knife, a cutting board, and a square foot of counter space. Miserable, I tried to make the preparation of the apples and the cutting of the cheese last forever. Then, startled, I glanced up as a voice registered against the background din.

"Mmm…apples and cheese! Now that sounds great." My first impression was color; a wildly patterned western shirt exploded under curly red hair. Her slim legs were tightly outlined by sparkling white denims, and, with her hands in her pockets, Darcy strolled slowly across the kitchen to admire my offerings.

She later told me that she had tracked my entrance, beguiled by what she saw as my air of serenity. Darcy said that she knew at that moment the graceful woman with long, dark hair was someone special.

All I knew was that my anxiety eased a little as she slowly approached, and a delicious new tension crept over me. We stood there awhile, making small talk, comparing the typical greasy, rich potluck food to the crisp tartness of green apples paired with the subtle flavors of the cheese. I broke away before I lost myself completely in her rich, chocolate-brown eyes and wove through the crowd to put my plate between platters of fried chicken and pizza rolls. Grabbing a thickly iced brownie, I headed back to the kitchen to find, I told myself, a less crowded spot.

I sternly focused on the fact that I was here to mingle, and I did speak to other women, but my eyes were drawn back to Darcy each time. I melted into a fantasy of being encircled by her warmth and protected by her power. I wondered over and over what it would be like to trace with my fingertips the outlines of her delicate features and be kissed by her alluring lips. She caught me staring boldly at her and I abruptly looked away. When I felt her eyes on me, I stood a little taller. But I didn't see her talk to a friend and point me out.

Meeting later in the hallway, we blocked foot traffic to and from the bathroom for nearly an hour while we shared our backgrounds and found we had much in common. Both younger children from large families, we each had alcoholic fathers and were recovering from childhood sexual abuse. We were both eclectic readers, loved music and movies, and gravitated toward animals.

Soon there was a general breakup of about half the crowd and, knowing I should leave, I stayed. Lisa and I finally met. She played piano and we all sang old rock-and-roll songs. Then Lisa played a song she had written for "my buddy, Darcy." It was a lovely, gentle lullaby about not fearing the night because someone trustworthy was near. I ached to be the one to keep the world safe for this beautiful, wounded woman.

Gradually I realized it was getting late, and when the next wave of women rose to leave, I grabbed my jacket too. It was easy to be sincere when I thanked Lisa for a special evening. I headed across the now misty street to my car, wondering if I would see Darcy again. Then I heard a faint voice behind me, calling my name.

Lisa had urged Darcy past her shyness and sent her out to give me her phone number. We stood talking for a few more minutes under the streetlight, mist forming a network of diamonds on Darcy's springy red curls. Then we exchanged numbers and said good night. I drove home with a grin wide enough to break my face and with the feeling of flapping, fluttering wings throughout my body.

Four years later I still shiver slightly when I replay that moment in my memory: my startled green eyes stare as cool, flaming Darcy slowly sauntered across the kitchen and into my heart. A plate of sliced tart apples and a variety of cheese wedges is still one of our mutually favorite bedtime snacks.

A Personal Decision

BY AMY J. SARUWATARI

When I turned 25 I succumbed to an ever-present curiosity about women by answering a personal ad. A local publication advertised a 900 number voice mail service for all categories of people from straight to gay. With my anonymity safely cloaked in voice mail disguise, I resolved to leave a message for a woman who was definitely seeking the company of another woman. The first voice that wafted into my ear was the only voice I needed to hear. She said sweetly that she was young, blond, and inexperienced with women, three traits I found agreeable, so I left my name and number. I assumed my chances of being called in return were slim, but she phoned me a few days later. She said she was compelled to call me since we both shared the first name, Amy.

Most of our conversations took place after 9 P.M., when she finished work. Many evenings I lay on my parents' couch, talking to Amy for hours on end. I felt an immediate connection with her, one that I had never experienced with anyone before. After two months of long-distance interaction it was time to set our first date. We decided to see a movie, *Robin Hood*, at a theater near Amy's apartment.

I remember driving to her place, mystified about what it was that two women did on a date with each other. Do I hold the door open for her? Will she expect me to kiss her good night? As I drove up to her building, a brick two-story the color of lime Jell-O, I squinted at the various doors, looking for apartment E. I climbed up a set of stairs and peered inside the first open door. There were two guys in shorts drinking beer. I knew I had the wrong place. Quickly I made my way over to the second set of stairs across the courtyard. Just as I reached the top step, I saw the back of her head through a screen door. I immediately noticed her wavy blond tresses. Her skin had the deep tone of a sun worshiper and her eyes were as blue as the a Caribbean sea. Amy had the all-American looks of a sorority sister. She was talking on the phone, but she motioned at me to come in and sit down.

I rubbed my sweaty palms on my torn jeans and turned away. All I kept thinking was, "Why would someone like her want to go out with me?" Amy finished the call, and we walked out the door. We decided to have dinner at a classy burger establishment, the kind of place where a waitress calls out your name when your order is ready, no reservations required. The first name called out was "Amy S.," and we walked up to the counter simultaneously. We both laughed at the coincidence of our last initials being the same, grabbed our salads, and sat down to talk. I raked my lettuce over with a fork, still nervous about the date.

"Don't think of this as a date, think of it as two friends going out," she said, and her casual manner allayed my fears.

During the course of dinner, the topic of middle names arose. "What is your middle initial?" I asked.

"J, which stands for Jean," answered Amy.

My jaw hurt from falling to the floor so fast. I thought she was kidding, that we couldn't possible have the same hideous middle name. I balked at this and jokingly asked to see her driver's license. Sure enough. She verified to me that we indeed had the same first name, middle name, and last initial. We concluded that our mothers were behind the name conspiracy. Over dinner and name games, her smile warmed my heart and her gaze ignited something deep inside of me, something primal and passionate.

We drove the short distance to the movie theater. The parking lot was wall-to-wall cars. Amy left the car to get tickets while I hunted for parking. After 20 minutes of driving in circles, I finally found a space and ran to the front of the theater to find her. She accused me of ditching her. I thought to myself that only a fool would abandon such a beautiful woman on a Saturday night. Inside, the theater was crowded and hot; too many bodies in a confined space. We found seats on the extreme left side of the dark room. Somehow I didn't mind being close to Amy for two hours. Watching the movie gave me a chance to enjoy her intoxicating perfume. I whispered my opinions about the movie into her ear just so I could smell her scent over and over again.

Robin Hood's British accent grew thinner and thinner as the movie wore on, but my feelings toward my date grew more and more intense. By the time the final credits rolled, we mutually agreed that the film was horrible. Unsure of what to do next, we decided to have cappuccinos at a quaint coffeehouse.

The night was cool and the air in the coffee bar was smoky. In spite of the fact that I had only spent hours with Amy, I felt like I had known her always. We conversed over steaming cups of coffee with an ease and candor that only close friends or intimate lovers share. The date concluded not with a kiss or even a handshake, but with a promise to continue seeing each other. That night I had a feeling that this was the beginning of a whole new journey. I hoped in my heart that Amy would be an integral part of that journey.

We have been together for almost six years and are planning to have a commitment ceremony in the near future. Never in my wildest dreams did I imagine that answering a personal ad would lead me to my true love, my soul mate, but it did. Because of taking the risk, my life would never be the same, and for that I'm grateful.

The Doorway

BY MEGHAN HERNER

I'm not really sure where the story of my coming-out begins. There are a lot of things that seem obvious now, but they weren't like that then. In the second grade I insisted on getting rainbow wallpaper.

"Are you sure you're not going to get tired of the rainbow?" my mom asked.

"I'm sure!" I was actually really sad when they took down the wallpaper a couple of years ago when I was in college.

There's something that needs to be understood about me before my story becomes interesting. I was the straightest person I knew. I lost my virginity at age 14 to a football player. Among my two good friends in high school, I was always the first to kiss and tell. This habit got me accepted to Lafayette College, voted by the *Princeton Review* to be the most homophobic school. As a freshman I entered the school as homophobic as my fellow classmates. I went to Lafayette to follow my boyfriend, who was a year older than me. He was the greatest thing on earth, and we were planning to marry.

We broke up sophomore year. I played around a lot afterwards. My new friend, Sue, was teaching me to be proud of who I was. Somehow I interpreted that to mean: sleep with whoever you want. As long as it was my choice, I had power. I was famous for going out with my friends, drinking, getting drunk, then disappearing with some guy.

Sue hated it when I did that. She said I had no respect for myself. We used to spend days not talking to each other after one of my little power trips. Sue became my best friend at Lafayette. We shared a lot with each other. She didn't belong there. I didn't feel like I belonged there either. Neither of us joined a sorority, which at a school like Lafayette is social death. We liked to hang out, drink, talk, play around. I acted like a kid, always goofing off and being silly. Sue was serious; she had never been shown how to play. We taught each other; we were good for each other.

The summer before my junior year I went to Spain. I was alone in a strange country, and only one person consistently wrote to me: Sue. I listened to a tape she sent me and got into the lyrics; it kept me company. While in Spain I discovered there was more to me than just drinking beer. I wasn't the party girl I thought I was. I returned home with a renewed sense of self, independence, and optimism.

Back at Lafayette nothing had changed. Most of the people were boring or stupid, in my opinion. One day Sue and I went to the grocery store and came back with a cat. He was sitting in the window next to the grocery store, and we talked each other into adopting him. Bud slept in Sue's dorm because she had a single. I began sleeping at her place so I could be with Bud. Sue and I were exceptionally close friends by then. I could tell her anything, and I usually did. I told her about all the guys I was sleeping with to feel my power as a woman with the right to choose…to sleep around. Sue and I were juniors and the afterlife (life after Lafayette) was becoming a reality. We adopted Bud not only because he was adorable, but also because we wanted an excuse to be together after graduation.

"You know, Sue," I said during our junior year, "every semester we've known each other we've become closer and closer friends." As an afterthought I asked myself, "Where can we go from here?" I was standing on the threshold of becoming a lesbian, but refused to look through the doorway. OK, maybe I didn't even see the door.

Sue and I would wrestle around in the hall. Then I would get drunk and sleep around. Everything was messed up. Sue would get angry and wouldn't call me. One time I went over to her room to coax her into talking with me.

"You don't know what I'm thinking," she said angrily.

"I bet I do," I responded. All of a sudden the idea occurred to me that Sue was a lesbian and she really liked me. I didn't say anything, though. We just hugged and made up, then carried on with our lives as usual.

It was during one of these fights that it happened. Sue was trying to explain to me how much it hurt her to watch me hurt myself like I did when I drank too much. We talked a long time, sitting on her couch, the candles burning and the daylight fading. We said harsh words and made each other cry. Then we held each other. We began to touch each other. I was really afraid but also excited. I remember thinking it was wrong, but it felt too good to stop. I hadn't been that sober or that sexually aroused during lovemaking for a long time. I felt like I was in junior high. Seven minutes in heaven with a boy, but don't let him get to second. Now it was a girl. It was Sue. I thought, *OK, I'll let her do X but not Y.* Then when she did Y, I said, *OK, but not Z.* I couldn't say no to her. It felt so good, and I had never experimented with a woman before. Two ridiculous thoughts went through my head. First I thought, *Sue's a lesbian but I'm not.* Then I thought, *When I'm older I can say I tried everything in college.*

We made love for a long time on that cool February day, only stopping when I realized I was late for work. Awkwardly I unmatted my bed-head and left the room, telling Sue I would come back after work. All throughout work I was completely distracted. I was right. Sue was a lesbian. I would just have to tell her I couldn't do it anymore. Couldn't we just be friends? I was still trying to figure out what to say when I saw her again.

I went directly to her room after work. I took a few uneasy steps toward her. Somehow I ended up cradled in her arms, wanting her to please me, wanting to please her again. We skipped classes the next day and every day for two weeks. We were together every moment. We laughed, we cried, we held, we touched, we danced, we loved. Finally, after the fifth day I accepted the fact that I wanted to be with Sue. It was the most important choice I've made in my life.

It took me a few weeks to come out to anyone else. Months later I could refer to myself as a lesbian. It took years to come out to my sisters and parents. After leaving Lafayette Sue and I took a road trip across the country. We stopped at every gay and lesbian bookstore on the way. We read history, coming-out stories, and erotica. We went to the Gay Pride celebration in San Francisco and marched in the dyke parade. I was still uncomfortable calling myself gay even then.

Since then we have moved to Seattle. Now I'm very out and won't be closeted at all. I work in a gay-run video store and live in a gay neighborhood. I celebrated my first Gay Pride Day where I was proud to be a dyke. Coming out to myself was hard to do in a small private school in Easton, Pa. But I'm just glad I have Sue to help me every step of the way.

It Started at a PJ Party

BY PAULA K. CLEARWATER

I think the most interesting aspect of my relationship with my partner is that we don't really know how long we have been together. We grew up in a small suburban town outside of Boston, our houses only about half a mile apart. Mine was a modest Cape containing our nuclear family of five. Hers was a rambling three-family farmhouse set up on an expansive knoll where she lived with her grandmother and family of boy cousins: a veritable Italian commune. Our neighborhoods were separated by the B&M Railroad track and a swampy section of the Ipswich River.

I remember her as being a loner. She was the only girl on the school bus who would sit sideways on the seat, her back up against the window like the boys, her legs slung onto the seat to prevent anyone from sitting with her. She carried her books on her hip. Despite the bitter New England winters, we were all forced to wear dresses to school in those days. Chris's mother made dresses for her and her younger sister. Her sister always looked as if she stepped out of a sunshiny milk commercial. Chris's dress hung shapelessly on her as if uninhabited, ignored. There was a defiance in her eyes that intrigued me, an independence that I admired. I recall now that I wanted to be her friend back then, though it would be years before we would connect.

In the seventh grade I became friends with her sister, who was my age. It was the late '60s, a time of camaraderie and exploration. Girls and boys hung out together in a group. We were the "freaks." We experimented with pot and acid, started a coffeehouse at a local church, organized to protest the war in Vietnam, and to boycott grapes with the migrant workers. We adventured in Harvard Square and drove to the ocean to bask in our budding sense of freedom. Chris stayed on the periphery of our clan. Her charisma was so strong that people would work hard to get past the austere persona she projected and would never let her completely disappear. I used to think that it was because of her cool exterior that people found her so attractive. It was as if she had seen it all. You wanted to get close to her because she knew the truth about things.

Our friendship blossomed on the night of Joyce Vecciarelli's pajama party. While the other girls were in Joyce's house watching television, doing up each other's hair, baking cookies, and talking about boys, Chris and I were sprawled out on the front lawn, gazing at the stars, talking about our life plans and about all the places we wanted to see. Our mutual love of travel galvanized a mutual intrigue.

All through high school Chris would pick me up in her father's car and we would drive around aimlessly, exploring our worlds, laughing at the same stuff. I liked her twisted perspective. She appreciated my compassion and trusting openness. We remained the best of friends despite my mother's efforts to keep us separate. She possessed a maternal intuition which correctly detected Chris's ability to easily influence me. But she never imagined the total seduction that would take place.

After graduation I went to college, then moved to California. Whenever Chris and I met back in our hometown during holidays it was like no time had passed between us. We easily picked up where we left off, feeling immediately simpatico.

I had relationships with men that I would describe as "successful relationships with endings." But I didn't know why they ended. They were good men. Some of them still remain friends. Ending our relationships was a mystery to me. When Chris and I reconnected again, I was living with a man I loved dearly. We lived together in a town next to where I had grown up. The relationship was ending for me. Once again I wasn't sure why. All I could identify was a nebulous, nameless yearning for something more. During this period Chris called out of the blue, inviting me to dinner.

As soon as our drinks arrived she announced that she had recently "come out of the closet." She thought I had always known she was gay. I told her I wasn't really surprised, but I had not assumed it. Then she said she realized as soon as she admitted to herself that she was a lesbian, she had always been in love with me. As in a scene from a sitcom, I blew my drink across the table.

We talked for four hours. I told her I was aware of wanting more from her, but I was never able to ascertain what "more" would look like. What "more" could there be to a deep, caring friendship? Then I told her I was in the process of moving out of the relationship I was in with the man I cared for. I didn't know what would happen if I chose to explore something more with her. The idea was exciting and scary. I did not want to set up an artificial arbitrary boundary in an effort to anticipate where I could go with it. If she was willing to take the ride, I'd be willing to board the train, not knowing if or when I might want to disembark.

It wasn't that the idea of being in a sexual relationship with a woman was new to me. There were several friends with whom I'd been so intimate that I thought, *If this was a man, we'd be married by now.* Though I needed time to sink into the idea of being in a full, sexual relationship with a woman, I knew before I finished my coffee that night that this was the thing I'd been searching for. More specifically, I'd been searching for Chris.

In a macabre twist of fate, the man I was involved with was diagnosed with terminal cancer. Not long after that Chris's father received the same news. We were devastated. I decided to stay with Alan and accompany him on this last leg of his earthly journey. It was a horrifying, yet strangely beautiful time. Chris and I spent time together whenever we could, taking much-needed drives through the countryside, watching sunsets, and sitting for hours overlooking the marshlands that surrounded our former hometown. It was a magical time of recollections, of renewed appreciation for life, of extracting an infinity from a single moment. We held each other through torrents of tears and massaged away the amorphous fatigue of having to stay alive, standing helplessly by while another's life drained away.

Within a month of each other, two years after they were diagnosed, my friend and Chris's father died. For weeks afterward I mulled around the eerily still aftershock, not knowing where to go from there. Chris was exhausted. It was becoming impossible for her to give herself to her job. I studied her one day, the lifeless way she held the piece of fruit she was eating, and said, "Let's take that trip we talked about on the night of Joyce Vecciarelli's pajama party! Let's get that Volkswagen van, load it up, and take off for a year to see the country!"

I didn't have to mention it twice. We used her last few paychecks and some of the money my generous Alan had left me, bought a trusty economical RV, put our stuff in storage, and took off.

The lusted-after life of beatnik transience we had dreamed about was not quite the idyllic panacea we imagined. There were many things to work out over those miles and during the hours of time alone. Each day presented hundreds of decisions regarding the need for regulating intimacy and alone-time, expectations both spoken and unspoken. Our trip turned out to be an intensive crash course in relating to one another from this new place. But about halfway through it became clear that we were looking for a place to settle down together.

That was almost ten years ago. Today, we sprawl out on the front lawn of our private acreage nestled in the White Mountains of Maine, gaze at the starlit night sky, and talk about the plans we have for our lives, all the things we want to experience, and all the places we want to see.

So What! Why Not?

BY TEDDI

It was a dark and stormy night.

It was! Why not? Everything was going perfectly until now…

After 18 years of marriage I was divorcing my husband. A professional, of course. Prominent in his field and religious community, of course. Jewish, of course.

After five years my lover was leaving me. She had decided to be "born again" as a Christian, instead of a "straight(?) lesbian." That's my term for her. Which she didn't find funny. It means a heterosexual who, to her great dismay, was madly in love with me. Another woman! Sometimes to my great dismay too. Sometimes to my great delight. Anyway, delight or dismay, she was leaving me. Other than, "*Oy vey*, the guilt!" I have no comment.

Some things you can fix. Some you shouldn't even try. I couldn't stop the rain. Maybe I could have stopped the divorce. But not our mutual anger and disappointment.

Maybe I could keep my lover. But that seemed to depend more on her mood than mine. Or on the stars. Something. Anything. But certainly not me.

So here I was joining a women's support group. It had started the previous week, but the facilitator let me join anyway (my money was still good.) So! I was here. Looking for a new woman and maybe a new life. I was here. And so was she. Sue. Sue had joined last week. On time. Probably the only time she ever was, as far as I can tell. But I didn't care. She was adorable, funny, and Jewish like me. And neither of us was going to be born again. I mean no disrespect to those who are. We're just not going to get together, not in this lifetime.

There were eight of us in the group. Eight and the facilitator—the paid professional. Some of were looking for understanding. Some for new friends. And some for a good time. Sue…OK, Sue and I were looking for all of the above. Maybe not as serious as we were supposed to be. But definitely with goals.

Here we were, outside of some lady's converted garage, standing in the rain, waiting for the group to begin. Maybe some of us were cruising the crowd. So? We were all trying equally hard not to get soaking wet waiting. We certainly all agreed the facilitator was either a control freak or a simple fool to not let us inside. She didn't think it was proper to let us in before "group" was scheduled to begin. Even out of the rain. It wasn't time to begin yet. I hadn't even met the lady yet, and I knew she was a fool! Too bad, but as it turned out, I was right. She liked rules. She didn't like Sue. Or me.

I don't like rules. Sometimes Sue doesn't either. OK, since I taught her not to, Sue doesn't like rules either. Anyway, we were here, women together, to take charge of our own lives, to make changes, to make things happen! Rules don't make things happen. It was raining. It was a dark and stormy night! Who cared about rules? We needed challenges, love, risks, love, a roof, a cup of coffee, tea, love, OK, hot chocolate! But not rules.

Some of us were standing pretty close. Sue came over. I said hello. She took one look at me, turned and walked away. Honest to God! She did!

It was a long, long, long time later that she told me she did think I was "sort of cute." But she saw that great big ring I still had on and figured she didn't need that kind of trouble.

It was not the best beginning. But it was typical for us. From then on everything that happened to us was one mix-up or miscommunication after another. And trouble. From then on we had nothing but trouble. Lots of love and loving, but trouble, trouble, trouble.

When my not-yet-ex kidnapped three of the kids and left me with $15 and the $1,000 rent due, that was only the beginning. (It *was* a nice ring, but it wasn't *that* big: I only got $1,000 for it.) Sure, that money, plus the $15 I already had, did help feed the kids he left behind. But Sue helped a lot more. It took a lot longer than the group lasted before I finally got on my feet.

Some cynics might think I stayed with Sue for her house and money. My ex (and I, until the divorce) had more of both. The money was nice, but was/is not why we stayed together for all these (almost 12) years.

We don't still make love all night, certainly not 15-20 times a night. We have jobs and the kids (it took lawyers and years, but finally they just came back because they wanted to). And there's the house to clean. Or not.

I'd like to say since that first wonderful night we knew we belonged together and we've never fought since. But that would be a crock. We fight all the time. But we never stop loving and respecting and wanting each other. And that's not bad. Not bad?

After our start it's a damned miracle! Not the results you would expect at all, especially from a group we were kicked out of. Members of the group were not supposed to become romantically involved. It was not a tough decision for us. We stayed together. We also stayed friends with a couple of other ex-group members. The facilitator? I heard she was run out of town. I heard she broke a couple of laws herself. Honest to God.

Of course it wasn't until we were introduced to each other formally, in group introductions (you know how groups work), that I knew for sure this beautiful face (yes, we're all a little chunky. So what?) was a wonderful, funny, Jewish (yes, by then, that mattered!), strong, good person. And I hoped (still do) to spend the rest of my life with her.

She sat on a couch. I sat on the floor between the couch and potted palm tree. At first I cried. My own story makes me sad. Then I spent the rest of the night laughing. Sue was one funny lady. I was smitten. She wouldn't go to "coffee" with me. I asked her to. But she had to take her ex-lover a birthday card. Of course that was strange. I never said she was perfect. Of course I was pissed.

I think it was after the next group. She was sitting in a big old chair and I was sitting on the floor at her feet. I asked her to go to bed with me. She swallowed her gum. Then we did, and did, and did. To tell the truth, I can't remember after which group that was. Or when exactly we got kicked out of the group because we were lovers. I never could remember dates. But boy, oh, boy, were we in love!

We were like teenagers. Awkward and alive and passionate and full of energy and laughter, and we didn't care much about anyone else, except my kids. We were always caring and careful, we thought, around them. We got the kids off to school, etc. etc. We did right by the kids. We spent lots of time with them and did the appropriate daytime stuff with them. Luckily the kids liked Sue too.

But the kids knew. Of course they did. They're not stupid. They grew up and out of her house. They went to college with her help.

All that came to happen after whichever group it was. All those endless phone calls became late night love-ins. And Sue and I finally knew for sure that in that poor excuse for a group we both did find just what we were looking for. Each other!

I knew first. She still says it was only because of that stupid ring that she walked away. Of course it doesn't matter. It's just more fun that way.

Touchdown!

BY HENRI

About 40 women were gathered at a Super Bowl potluck in a suburban neighborhood. Our hostess had recently come out after a long marriage. Her home reflected a static life of housewifery, with its proper living room studded with knickknacks and framed photos of her children and grandchildren. But in the back room she was surrounded by lesbians who came to watch football or to cruise, or to be with friends or meet new ones.

During halftime the jocks left the television to check out the food and drinks. It gave us social ones a chance to talk. I asked a young woman I knew how her research into San Francisco sex clubs was progressing. She launched into her latest adventures. I kept drawing her out by asking naive questions; she was providing unique entertainment to our mostly middle-class, middle-aged group. Then I heard laughter that rose above everyone else's in its energy, length, and openness. Where was this laughter coming from?

A quiet, white-haired woman I hadn't met before was sitting on the couch. I sat down beside her and we introduced ourselves. She was a tall, big-boned, older dyke. She wasn't accustomed to hearing such open discussions of kinky sex, she told me. Would she like to hear more? I asked, flirtatiously. This brought on the laughter again. I loved hearing it.

She had come to the football party with a mutual friend of ours. This was her first potluck. She was beginning to get out and meet lesbians after recovering from the end of a long relationship. I didn't dwell on the fact that I was still in one, nor that my much younger partner was in the dining room with another group who preferred playing board games to watching football. Because I felt restless, unfulfilled, mismatched with my lover, I was always flirting with women. It seemed a natural part of my personality. This woman did not flirt back. She asked me questions and really cared to hear the answers. I liked her mix of seriousness and humor.

About five months later we met again at a pool party potluck. I felt an attraction to her and took every opportunity to be in her company. One of her skills was massage, and when she casually reached down to rub my back—I was sitting on the floor at her feet—I moved closer. She noticed this. As she told me later, she too felt an attraction and was surprised at my response to her touch, but was unsure of what to do because I was in a relationship.

Our mutual friend was quite aware of what was going on. During the ensuing months, she would come to my house to visit, look into my eyes, tell me how unhappy I looked, and ask if all was well with my partner and me. To this other woman, she continually extolled my virtues. Our friend believed we were a good match and wanted us together.

A year later the pool party was held again. My partner begged off attending so I went early. The woman was there, sitting by the side of the pool. I immediately sat next to her, and we spent the next hour talking, oblivious to everyone. Later, we attempted to stay apart just to maintain some sense of decency, though no one seemed to find our behavior suspicious. But we continually gravitated to each other during the evening. When she looked at me, her gaze seemed to penetrate into my soul. I would have followed her anywhere at this point, but she did not seem to want to lead me anywhere as much as just be in my company.

A few days later I left on a trip along the coast by myself. I needed to get away and think. Everywhere I went I imagined how it would be if she was with me. Finally I wrote her a letter and told her how I felt about her. I suggested we could have a relationship separate from the one I was in—it has been my utopian vision that open relationships can work, but I've never found anyone willing to experiment. When I returned we met, and she gave me a full body hug. I loved her hugs; they were enhanced by her experience in massage work and her belief in the positive aspect of touch. Then she said I would have to choose, to make a decision between her and my partner.

We met many times to talk and get to know each other better. I found that she complemented with her spiritual nature my more materialist and earthbound concerns; she calmed me down and drew me out. She brought me back from becoming the hermit that I felt myself evolving toward as I aged. As we became more intimate, I could no longer deny the truth of what was happening. I told my partner, and we broke up.

My new lover and I have committed ourselves to each other. We exchanged rings and statements at the beach, surrounded by unknowing strangers. This was the first relationship I'd had in which such an exchange took place. Then we had a celebration party and invited as many friends as would fit into my apartment. We are both in our 60s, and we are both fully committed to each other for the rest of our lives. We don't yet live together, but we plan to in two years when we retire.

Happy Birthday

BY CHRISTY CRAMER

I don't remember the first time I met Lorrie, but my mother told me about it. Lorrie remembers, but then she is eight years older than I. Two years old is sort of young to remember introductions, and, of course, Lorrie's and my relationship really began many years later.

We've been together for 13 years. That is my estimate. According to Lorrie, it's been a few years less than that. But in my mind our first date was on my 15th birthday. We celebrate our anniversary as being 13 years, because when we chose our anniversary she got to pick the date, and I got to decide the number of years we celebrate. As far as I'm concerned, we've been together 13 years in August.

Here is how our first encounter was related to me by both my mother and Lorrie. I was two. Lorrie was visiting with her cousin who occasionally baby-sat me. I just stood and stared at Lorrie. They couldn't get me to play or talk. After this first meeting I kept asking for Lorrie. My mother said she would get me a "Lorrie doll," but that wasn't what I was looking for. I wanted to see Lorrie.

As my childhood years went by, Lorrie played an important role. She lived two doors down from my family, and we saw each other often. Lorrie walked her dog in the fields behind our house, and my friends and I often joined her. Sometimes she played kickball and monster ball with us. She was the best kicker! I remember being amazed. She could kick the ball four houses away. That was farther than any of the boys could kick. I thought she was incredible and really cool. Needless to say, I had a crush on her even back then.

When I was 11, my family moved away. Every time I visited my friend Jenny, who still lived in that neighborhood, I would drag her over to see Lorrie. I never told Jenny, but the main reason I visited her house was to visit Lorrie. That was the highlight of the trip.

Lorrie and I did eventually lose touch for a while. Probably from the time I was 12 until I was 14. Then I started writing to her and calling her. I'm sure I was a pest. I mean, why would a 22-year-old want a 14-year-old hanging around? Eventually, however, I won her over. She started to think of me as a little sister, and after months of persuasion, she finally agreed that we could spend an afternoon together. That first afternoon was my 15th birthday.

It wasn't until years later that we realized my birthday get-together had been a date to me. I wasn't out to myself back then, but, looking back, it seems so clear. We went to the Ground Round, a steak-and-burger place, for dinner. I was a bundle of nerves. Not only had I never gone out to eat with my parents, I had such a crush on Lorrie. My face was red, and the entire afternoon I could hardly look at her when we spoke. I didn't want her to see me eat. I just wanted her to like me and felt awkward. I still thought she was extremely cool and, in my mind, I just didn't add up. After dinner we went to a game room. I had a terrific time, and to this day I still have the leftover tokens we didn't use.

Lorrie was the type who wore faded jeans, a white T-shirt, and a black leather jacket. She also wore black leather boots. She had medium-length brown curly hair and gorgeous brown eyes. She drove a beat-up old Nova and could even work on the car herself. I had never seen a woman working on a car before. I was attracted to Lorrie not only because of her looks and mechanical skills, but also because she was the first person to treat me like my feelings mattered. We talked easily, and she seemed to really care about what I said.

Strange as it may seem, I was the initiator in our relationship. The first time Lorrie kissed me was because I had been coming on to her for a quite some time. I didn't realize that was what I was doing, but I got the desired results whether my actions were conscious or not.

I think it could be said that I knew Lorrie was the one for me when I first saw her at the age of two. Children have a sixth sense about these things. The afternoon of my 15th birthday began the wonderful relationship that we still share today.

Gay America Online

BY BARBARA

When I agreed to write my own story, I began to realize how meaningful the word *beginnings* was for me at this point in my life. At the age of 51 and after 25 years of a relatively happy marriage, the unthinkable happened. I fell in love for the first time in my life.

I have three wonderful young adult children, two sons and a daughter. I had it all: a wonderful husband, children, a lovely home in suburbia with the white picket fence. Who could ask for more? Yet I knew something was missing from my life. Little did I know what that missing piece of my life would be.

I had returned to working full-time when my youngest child was in junior high school, so I didn't really have a career per se. I wasn't satisfied with my job, and when all three children were in college I started my own home billing business. I bought a computer, printer, and fax machine. In preparation for starting my business, I needed to learn all about my computer. I signed onto America Online, sharing this enthusiasm with my kids. Then one November evening while working alone in the basement I ventured into that forbidden place: The Gay and Lesbian Forum on AOL.

For no apparent reason I convinced myself it was out of curiosity that I entered a room called Women's Space and just watched the interaction between all these women. They were all busy typing, using symbols foreign to me, and it was all I could do just to read what they were all saying to each other. I had a difficult time keeping up with the conversations, so I just sat back and "listened." I met a couple of women who told me about a Sunday evening group called Fine Wine for women over 40! *How wonderful*, I thought.

So that's where I ventured the following Sunday evening. I was only on my computer for two weeks and still knew little about it when I met the love of my life. I was visiting the Fine Wine room and attempting to join in the dialogue with something worth sharing when I received an "instant message." I had no idea how this person sent me a message, but there I was, conversing with a stranger from Massachusetts. She advised me to be careful of what I said and to not give out too much information about my personal life. *Good advice*, I thought, and thanked her for clueing me in.

Her name was Jean, and she was 42 years old. We continued to communicate through E-mail for weeks, although it seemed like years. We knew everything you would ever want to know about someone's life: family, friends, jobs, kids, dogs, likes and dislikes and whatever. We shared the same values, and although we were raised in different environments, we respected our differences. Communication is very important to me, and, unlike my husband and I, Jean and I had the ability to communicate on so many levels. And that made her very attractive to me. I felt as if I transcended time for all the intensity our conversations enveloped. We exchanged pictures and telephone numbers and began talking almost every day for weeks.

After sharing with my new friend many personal and intimate details of my life, I started experiencing very real feelings for her. At first these feelings frightened me, and I had a hard time understanding them. But they were real, and I finally had to admit that I fell in love with Jean on the computer before we ever met in person. How is this possible? Well, it is possible because it happened to both of us!

I had had feelings for one other woman in my life two years earlier and was still trying to understand the meaning of it when I met

Jean. Needless to say, I wanted to meet this person who was tugging on my heart. And eventually we arranged a meeting. I took a day off and shortly before Christmas of 1994, and I drove to Massachusetts for "some early Christmas shopping" with my new "computer friend," I explained to my family.

The trip took four hours from Long Island, and I arrived at her door just in time for breakfast. When Jean opened the door I knew we would be friends. I didn't know how to react, so being the professional woman I was at work, I extended my hand. She just smiled, gave me a little laugh, then reached out and hugged me. I was more embarrassed than anything. I was also nervous about meeting Jean because she knew I had feelings for her, had never been with a woman before, nor had I ever kissed one.

Jean was married for 23 years to a man, had no children, but was in three lesbian relationships over the course of her marriage for brief periods at a time. We agreed ahead of time that neither of us would do anything we weren't ready for or was uncomfortable with. So I did feel safe in her home and in her presence. Jean prepared a delicious breakfast and we talked for a while. It felt as if I had known her all my life.

Then it happened. We were in the living room and she gave me an intense hug. It was with great warmth and comfort, such as I had never experienced before. I felt a sudden surge go through my body, and I seemed to have melted into her in some way. I can't even describe the feeling, but it went through me, it was electric. Jean must have sensed it because she whispered softly in my ear, "Do you want to go upstairs?"

I was a little surprised by the question, but I knew it was what I wanted too. She took my hand and led me upstairs to her bedroom. Gently, she sat me down on the side of the bed and looked at me with eyes so loving, they would melt any heart. She leaned down and kissed me on the lips. My first lesbian kiss, and I can still re-member how wonderful it felt. I heard the bells and whistles, and I knew I was home! She took my top off and then my bra. I helped her along the way until she reached for the button on my jeans. Then I freaked out. I grabbed her hand and instinctively pushed it away. After all, I had limits too!

"I can do it myself," I explained and retreated to the bathroom. I am very shy about my body. Only one other person had seen me naked, and that was my husband. So after the shock wore off and having her turn away from me, I jumped into her bed and covered myself quickly.

We proceeded to make love, and I will never forget the magic of how she felt being so close to me. Although I felt awkward making love with a woman, it seemed to come naturally as time went on. After 25 years of 15-minute sex, you could imagine my surprise at learning what two people in love could do for three hours! I thought I died and went to heaven. I have never felt such love in all my life, and the whole experience was extremely emotional. I still consider my relationship with Jean as sacred, and one that I treasure to this day.

I returned home that same day, with a wreath for my home—the Christmas shopping—and a love in my heart that grows every day. In January of the new year, I told my twin sister, Pat, that I wanted to separate from my husband because I had fallen in love with some-one. She wasn't surprised because she had known for years that I wasn't happy in my marriage. She wanted to know his name!

I said, "You mean her name."

And she responded, "Are you coming out of the closet?"

Almost simply I replied, "Yes, I am out of a closet that I didn't even know I was in."

I told my husband about Jean and asked for a separation and a di-vorce. I was honest with my children. I had to be. You don't just leave a marriage after 25 years for no reason, and I had a good one. My children were more upset with me for breaking up their happy home than with the fact that their mom was a lesbian. I moved out of my home by summer and into an apartment. After Jean's husband moved out and they separated, I moved to Massachusetts to live with Jean.

Jean and I are now both divorced, and my ex-husband has re-married. I am still good friends with him and his new wife. The relationship with my children, although strained, is getting better as time goes by.

The "beginning" of my new life has not been easy for me or Jean. We both left our husbands for each other. I had difficulty adjusting to a single life, with no real means of support, except an occasional job here and there. Jean has had a career for over 20 years, and I am still trying to fit in somewhere. Although Jean and I have recently separated, I know our separation is only temporary since we both needed to take time to grow in ways that will make our relationship stronger. She is my best friend. More importantly, we are still very much in love. I have many new "beginnings" with a new life and a new love. Who could ask for more? I have found the "more" in more ways than one.

Tequila in a Rainstorm

BY SANDRA J. FITZPATRICK

The small red-and-white plane rolled across the flat, tightly vegetated tundra, gently lifting above the valley nestled among the rugged, glaciated mountains. We stood watching it slowly disappear, the awesome quiet settling in around us. As far as the eye could see there were tundra and mountains. I couldn't believe we were really here, alone, in the middle of the wilderness.

I thought about everything that had led up to this moment. It was only on our second date that Maria casually mentioned her plan to go to the Brooks Range, north of the Arctic Circle. She was planning a trip to the Gates of the Arctic National Park and was looking for someone to go with her. She came to Anchorage to work for the summer and had allotted two weeks for this trip before she returned to law school. As she pulled out her maps to show me where it was, she turned to me and said, "Hey, Sandy, why don't you come with me?"

Sure. Fly in a small plane to the middle of grizzly territory in a remote wilderness, all of which would scare me to death! What I said was, "Sure, that sounds great!"

The more we talked about it, the more I actually began to believe that I could really do this. I was an ex-Girl Scout. I was raised on a ranch in Texas. I was experienced in camping and the outdoors. How hard could it be?

I told my friends about my plans to go to the "Brooks" with Maria. They couldn't believe it. Me!? The crème de la femme!?!

Everyone had advice or a story to tell, mostly about grizzlies. I decided to look up the facts for myself. The "Bear Facts" brochure published by the Alaska Department of Fish and Game gives this advice:

Let the bear know you are human. Talk to the bear. Never imitate the bear sounds or make a high-pitched squeal. If a bear actually makes contact, surrender. Play dead. If the bear continues biting you long after you assume a defensive posture, it likely is a predatory attack. Fight back vigorously.

Right. Fight back vigorously. As if at that point it'd matter.

And now here I was, standing on the tundra, with no time for second thoughts; we needed to get settled before evening. My heart was still pounding, and my muscles were tense, even with all the Dramamine I had taken for the flight. It had taken several doses to convince me to climb into the little two-seater Piper Cub that had flown me here.

Jerry, our bush pilot, reminded me of a younger version of my dad, who had been a pilot in the Air Force. He had the same no-nonsense look about him, that same lean and wiry build. Maria found Jerry through an ad in the Alaska guidebook. His Piper Cub only held two people, himself and one passenger. He had flown us one at a time from Bettles, an edge-of-the-Arctic town of about 40 people, to a remote cabin hidden in the trees on the Tinayguk River.

Jerry flew Maria in first, dropped her off with half of our food and gear, then returned for me and the rest of the supplies. He left her alone in the middle of the Brooks Range with only the eerie silence for company. She stood out on the tundra, shotgun in hand, watching, waiting, listening for any rustle, any movement that would mean "grizzly." I arrived two hours and six Dramamine later.

Trying to be brave, I took a deep breath, smiled, and said, "So, how's the cabin?"

She looked at me sheepishly, saying, "I don't know. I was too nervous to go down to the cabin by myself. You can't see in front of you in those willows and bushes. It was just more than I could handle."

I loved her for admitting that. Somehow it made me feel better knowing I wasn't the only one who was scared. "You poor thing. You waited here all by yourself while Jerry came back and got me. It must have been awful." I hugged her. "Come on. Let's go check it out together."

We gathered our packs and boxes of food, ready to venture into grizzly territory. I kept telling myself I had to do this; after all, Jerry was gone, leaving us here alone for two weeks. For Maria, this trip was the culmination of a lifetime dream. For me, it was a crazy, spontaneous response to a beautiful woman.

We tromped through the brush and willows, hollering, "Hey, bear! Hey, bear!" as we walked. The thought of walking into a grizzly made it hard to keep up the requisite number of "Hey, bears" I was expected to contribute. The theory of the grizzlies is simple—if you let them know you are there, and if you don't surprise them, they won't hurt you. Bears are afraid of humans and don't want any contact with us. The key word here, of course, is *theory*. So we kept up our clapping and "hey, bear"-ing through the willows to the cabin. We made it, finally, after what seemed an eternity.

The cabin was a darling sod-roofed affair nestled among the pine and birch trees. It sat on a peninsula of land surrounded by a fresh water stream on one side and the glacier fed Tinayguk River on the other. Right out of *Northern Exposure*. Perfect! On closer inspection I saw the claw marks on the front door, the bear fur on the pine tree next to the cabin, and the caribou antlers and bones on the ground outside the door. Then when I peeked inside the cabin I saw a two-inch layer of silt covering the floor. Heavy rains and melting snow in the spring must have flooded the cabin, leaving the glacier silt behind. Perfect.

But I decided to make the best of it. "I guess we could put our sleeping bags on those bunk beds to sleep on and…what?" I couldn't help but notice the look on Maria's face as she surveyed the place.

She was frowning. "Spiders! I can't stand spiders. There are bound to be tons of them in here. Just look at this place. We can't stay here. There must be spiders everywhere!"

Butches never cease to amaze me. They can be so tough, so calm, in so many different situations. You just never know what their particular Achilles' heel might be. I just discovered Maria's.

"It's OK, honey. We'll think of something. Why don't we go look around outside first?"

She gratefully accepted.

Still worried about running into bears, we took the shotgun with us to explore the area around the cabin. We promptly found fresh bear scat and knelt down to examine it. The pile was huge! About as big around as a jumbo cinnamon roll. A dark brown one full of berries and leaves. (Cinnamon rolls haven't held the same appeal for me since.) I was instantly nervous and grateful we had the shotgun with us. As we walked back to the cabin, I thought about how we got the gun.

Planning this trip began in earnest on our third date (remember, we're on lesbian time here). Maria got out her backpacking list and said, "It's taken me years to compile this list through trial and error from years of backpacking while I was a park ranger in the Sierra Nevadas. It's everything you would ever need for any trip in the wilderness."

"You were a park ranger? I didn't know that."

"Yeah, it's great stuff to impress other dykes when you're out drinking. 'Hey, did you know I used to be a park ranger?' Very high on the butch scale, don't you think?"

"At least a ten!" I laughed and looked at the list. It seemed very short to me for a two-week trip to the middle of nowhere, but Maria assured me it was complete. I was not convinced. It didn't even have chocolate on it!

She patiently explained to me, "On a trip like this, everything has to be carefully planned. The only food and supplies we'll have is what we take with us. And we have to consider the dimensions and weight because everything will have to be flown in. Don't worry, I'll take care of all the food and gear."

I still felt I had to put in my two cents worth. "Okay. But be sure to bring plenty of tampons and chocolate. The good kind, not the cheap stuff—the chocolate, I mean. And I like pecans, not peanuts. I hate peanuts in chocolate. Those turtle things are my favorite. You know, the caramel and the pecans. Oh, yeah, and don't you think we should take a gun in case we run into grizzlies?"

The word "gun" of course caught Maria's attention. She sat back, looked at me thoughtfully, and said, "Yeah, I guess we should. We are going into bear country. Do you know anything about guns? Do you know where we could get one?"

I did know a little about guns, being raised on the Texas ranch and all, but I didn't know which kind we should take or where to get one. "Sure, I know all about them. I'll be in charge of getting us a gun."

So I began my search for a gun. I struck gold during a board meeting at work, of all places. Fred was a gun enthusiast and instructor. He said he'd be happy to loan me a "870 over/under, collapsible stock, pump-action shotgun that would shoot bear slugs." I nodded thoughtfully as if I knew what he was talking about. "That sounds like a good choice," said I. "When can I pick it up?"

He slapped me on the back like I was one of his hunting buddies. "I'll be instructing a class at the rifle range on Saturday. Why don't you come by then?"

"Great!" I grinned stupidly again, my heart racing with the thought of having to deal with a shotgun that shot "bear slugs," whatever that was. And "pump-action!" All I could think of was Linda What's-Her-Name in *Terminator II*, pumping that shotgun with one hand, blasting away. I called Maria with the good news. I had found us a gun.

Saturday came all too quickly. As we parked in front of the building, I took a deep breath. Maria was exceptionally quiet.

"Let's get this over with," I said. Maria nodded, and we went in and found Fred's class. I peeked in the door and nearly fainted. The room was full of men! I ducked back but it was too late. Fred had spotted me.

"Come in, come in. Hey, glad you made it. I've got the shotgun right here. Now you know all about these things, right? You push this button here to collapse the stock, and you may want to do that since you're so short. Ha-ha. So without the stock you want to shoot from the hip. You won't be able to aim or anything, just wait till they get real close, then fire away. They say to shoot for the shoulder to knock them down. Ha-ha. I'm not so sure about that. I've heard the only way to really stop a grizzly is to hit them in the neck, and that's kind of hard because they usually have their head down when they're charging. Ha-ha. So here's the safety. On. Off. And this button opens the chamber so you can load. This baby holds eight slugs. So fire away. Ha-ha. Any questions?"

I was trying to watch everything he was showing me and keep my cool at the same time. I'm not sure I succeeded. I said, "No, I think I've got it. Just to be sure, why don't you run by the chamber thing again?"

Fred ran quickly through the opening and closing of the chamber one more time, then said, "Well, good luck. Have a nice trip."

We put the gun in the trunk of the car and stared at it. Neither of us had seen anything like it except on television or in movies. We just looked at each other and drove to the rifle range. Trembling, we only managed to shoot the gun once.

Thinking about the shotgun made me smile. The smile quickly disappeared, however, when we got back to the cabin. What to do about all the silt and spiders? I could see Maria was reluctant to venture into the gloomy mess, so I went in and took a better look.

The cabin was about 8 by 8, with a wooden shelf on one side with old rusted pots and pans stacked on it. There were two large wooden bunk beds and a small wooden table by the door. I checked the door. It was about six inches thick and looked like it could keep out a grizzly. There were two small windows on either side, letting in light, but too small for a bear to crawl through. All estimates were based on my tremendous knowledge of bears, of course.

I saw some rolls of plastic sheeting and decided to roll them out on the floor to cover the dirt when I had a brainstorm. "I know. We can sleep in our tent! We can set it up on the floor of the cabin and the tent will keep the spiders out!"

Maria grinned. "That's a great idea. Then we can take it down during the day so we can move around in here."

We got to work. I moved the rusted pans out of the way to make room for our two pots, two plates, two spoons, and two cups. Then I unpacked the tent and our sleeping bags and set them on one of the bunks out of the way. We both hung our clothes on nails sticking out from the wood beams overhead. Maria sorted food for the evening and fixed up a makeshift table outside to cook on.

We soon discovered that we worked very well together. We both liked setting up camp, and we enjoyed a comfortable silence around each other. When we felt we had done enough, we decided to go out and take another look at the valley.

We took the shotguns and binoculars and walked back up the path, ringing our bells we had unpacked to let the bears know we were coming, and yelling, "Hey, bear!" as we went. I noticed this time it only took two minutes to make the trek.

We picked a hill that rose away from the tundra. Neither of us spoke as we stepped carefully from one cushiony tussock to another. We finally reached the top and looked around. We could see forever from there. We were in the middle of a long, narrow valley dissected by the winding, glacier-fed Tinayguk. On every side were purple and gray knife-edged mountains sloping down the tundra. It was early August, but the tundra was already the color of fall; bright reds and oranges surrounded us. The only trees were birch and pine in the ravine next to the river where our cabin sat. It was completely silent.

"This is beautiful. I could sit and look for hours, but I'm exhausted. I feel like crashing right here." Maria stretched out on the cushiony ground. The tundra was covered with small, tightly interlaced plants that made the ground soft and spongy. "This is much better than sleeping with spiders!" Maria said before curling up on her jacket and closing her eyes.

The ground looked like it was covered with just one type of plant, but on closer inspection, I could see an amazing variety of delicate flowers, mosses and lichens. Still nervous about bears, I stood guard with the shotgun while Maria napped. As I stood there on the hill, a thousand miles from any civilization, the silence began to make room for the sounds around me. The birds, deciding we were no threat, began to go about their business of living.

There was a colony of Arctic ground squirrels on the hill next to the one we were resting on. One squirrel would stand watch, just as I was doing, while the others ran up and down the trails their little feet had cut through the tightly packed vegetation. They would run and eat, run and eat, always moving along the little trails. The trails crisscrossed the tundra, adding a deep brown outline to the reds and oranges. Later Maria and I learned to trust the little guards' judgment about bears and looked for them up on the hill as we emerged from the cabin every morning.

As I stood guard over Maria, my thoughts drifted to when we first met. I smiled as I thought about that day. It was June 18, almost solstice. We were at an outdoor barbecue at a friend's house. It was a beautiful, sunny day, and my best friend, Judith, had come over to talk me into going. I was recovering from a broken heart and didn't want to go, but Judith convinced me. I pulled my long wavy gray hair up into a ponytail under my baseball cap and announced I was ready.

I almost regretted giving in to Judith when we arrived at a backyard full of youngish women I didn't know, but I relaxed when I recognized a few faces. I pulled out my lawn chair and sat back to catch some rays. I was halfheartedly engaged in conversation with the woman sitting next to me when Maria arrived.

She was mesmerizing. To say she was all, dark, and handsome would be an understatement. Tall to me anyway, at 5 feet 8 inches, with short dark curly hair. She had a look about her that commanded attention. Her eyes especially. They were deep brown, large, and framed with beautiful long lashes. Her eyes swept the group of women, sizing everyone up in one glance. And her smile—full lips sliding easily over perfect, even teeth. A friend of ours later described her as "feature for feature, the most attractive woman I know." And it's true. Her hands, their expressive long fingers covered with distinctive silver jewelry, were a femme's dream come true. She was mixed-race, with very light skin. With my Italian skin tanned to my midsummer golden hue, I was actually darker.

"What are you smiling at?" Maria was awake from her nap on the tundra.

"Oh, I was just sitting here thinking about the day we met."

Maria smiled. "You mean at the premier lesbian barbecue in Anchorage?"

I walked over and sat next to her. "Yes. Where you and all the other dykes were showing off throwing Frisbees."

"Well, you didn't seem to mind. You couldn't take your eyes off me. I saw you watching me," she grinned.

I gave her a playful shove, "I couldn't help it! You were so athletic and graceful, jumping over the fence like that to catch the Frisbee."

"I did that on purpose. I was showing off." She laughed.

"Well, it certainly caught my attention." I leaned closer. "When did you notice me?"

"I really noticed you when you were 'holding court,' as Judith called it. Sitting there in the middle of all those attractive, younger women, talking so easily, answering all their questions. I was impressed with how quick-witted you were. And the way you laughed with your head tossed back. I thought that was sexy as hell."

"What was it you said again?" 'I hear all these women flirting with you and carrying on. I just want you to know they're all talk, but I'm interested.' I knew that was a line, but by God, it worked!" I laughed.

"Is that why you came up to me after the party and asked me...how did you put it?...'You know, I'm sure you know what you're doing when it comes to having a good time. I'm just curious if you know what you're doing emotionally as well?' That really threw me off guard!"

I smiled at her. "I'm glad you took my question seriously. When you told me you had relationship problems in the past but were really working on it, I could see the vulnerability in your face. I knew then there was more to you than just charm and good looks." I kissed her tenderly. "Talking about our recent breakups and not wanting to get involved again…it seemed we were on the same page. That was when I knew I would see you again."

"And you did, didn't you? Now here we are sitting on the tundra in the Brooks. And I'm glad." She stood and stretched. "Hey, we better get back to the cabin. It's beginning to cloud up."

It began to rain just as we reached the cabin. I collapsed on my sleeping bag on one of the bunks while Maria fixed supper. We celebrated our first night with macaroni and cheese and a shot of tequila.

We spent the next several days taking short hikes exploring the area. We gradually felt ourselves tuning in with the rhythm of the tundra. Each day started out hot and sunny and ended with fast-moving clouds and a quick rainstorm. Every evening we ate at our little table, snug and secure in our cabin, watching the rain.

One day we hiked to the top of a hill and sat silent and still for hours, scanning the landscape for movement with our binoculars, seeing nothing. Jerry had told us there was a large pack of wolves in the area, led by a huge black. He had seen them several times. But after a week of hiking and scanning the horizon for movement, we were beginning to feel a little discouraged. We hadn't seen there pack, and today was no different. As we gathered our gear to go back to the cabin, Maria said, "Let's howl like wolves. Maybe they are here and they will answer us."

"Really? They'll howl back? Won't they attack us?" I was unsure.

"No, wolves aren't dangerous. I worked one summer in Montana for the university tracking wolves by radar. We howled several times and always got a response."

We threw our heads back and howled as loud as we could. "A-a-ahwo-o-o!"

Suddenly a full-grown moose jumped up from where she had been lying in a shallow hollow. She took off running across the tundra, wildly turning her head from side to side trying to see these strange-sounding "wolves." With her long, lanky legs, it took her less than a minute to run across the tundra into the protection of the trees by the river. We were stunned. We had sat, not 20 feet from her, straining our eyes to see some wildlife and hadn't caught a glimpse of her.

"She was right under our feet. That could have been a bear!" I was shaking so hard I could hardly stand.

"Let's get back to the cabin!" Both of us knew if it had been a grizzly that close we wouldn't have had enough time to chamber slugs and fire the shotgun.

We prepared dinner in silence, both of us still thinking about the moose. I realized that we could get seriously hurt out here. And watching Maria, the thought of losing her made my eyes fill with tears. I knew how much I loved her.

I looked up from my spaghetti. "Maybe we should shoot the shotgun again. Just to remember how."

"Yeah, maybe. I don't know, though. Shooting that shotgun was just as scary as being startled by the moose."

"I remember when we went to the rifle range to shoot it. I was shaking so hard I could hardly shoot. And you! You should have seen the look on your face!"

"At least you've been around guns before. I haven't," Maria answered.

She was right. I used to go hunting and target shooting on my dad's ranch with my brothers all the time. But that was with a .22 single shot, not an 870 pump-action shotgun. "I was surprised I even hit the target. Especially shooting from the hip like that."

"I was impressed. A femme like you shooting an awesome assault weapon. I think I fell in love with you right then." She grinned at me from across the table.

"I was a little impressed myself." I leaned closer. "We sure did scare that moose, didn't we? Geez, she was fast."

"I had no idea we sounded so menacing." We laughed, and Maria got up to get the limes and tequila. It was hard to believe we were so easy with each other. There's nothing that will make or break a relationship quicker than a trip together, but this trip was proving how compatible we were.

"Remember our first date?" I asked.

"How can I forget? It was great." She set the tequila down between us.

"I don't know about you, but I was full of doubt. I was still hurting over my breakup and was unsure if I wanted to get involved again, even if it was only for a summer fling." I cut the lime into quarters. "I remember parking out front by the fountain waiting for you. I was really nervous. Then when you came out you looked like you had been crying and I asked you if you were OK."

"My ex had just sent back all the pictures of us together and everything I ever gave her. It was kind of hard."

I nodded. "Breaking up is tough. To be honest, I almost didn't go, but then I thought maybe I'd feel better if I did."

"I'm glad you did. It was better being out with you than home by myself feeling bad."

"Much better," I smiled. "I took you to that hole-in-the-wall restaurant with the best Thai food in town. I told you I really didn't like to date, I preferred just hanging out with someone to get to know them. I've had some real dates from hell."

She laughed at that and looked at her watch. "Well, it's been an hour so far, how are we doing?"

"That's exactly what you said then! That was so cute!"

Maria reached over and took my hand. "Afterward we drove to the bar where your friend was playing, and all your friends came over to say hello and look me over." She just shook her head and said, "You Sagittarians! You're all alike. You know everyone!"

"I guess I do. I've lived in Anchorage for 20 years."

"We sat on the couch listening to the band play the last set. I felt like we were in a fishbowl. But when you started stroking my arm, I stopped caring," she said as she caressed my arm.

That night we reenacted our first date as best we could within the constraints of long underwear, sleeping bags, and a tent!

The next day we hiked to the top of our lookout hill for a picnic. We were relaxing, enjoying the sun, when Maria saw something move on the tundra above our cabin.

"I see something! I think it's a bear." She was looking through the binoculars.

"Where? Oh, I see it. Is it a black bear?" I whispered. I didn't want to scare it off, whatever it was.

She handed me the binoculars. "It's the wolf!" It was the black wolf Jerry had told us about. It was huge. As I watched he lifted his head and looked right at us. He knew we were there. Then he began circling, sniffing, and pawing the ground. It looked like he was hunting for mice. He took his time about it, occasionally looking our way. After about ten minutes, he trotted off.

"All that summer I spent doing wolf research, I never saw a wolf. This was my first one. I can leave now feeling satisfied," Maria sighed.

We walked back to the cabin, thrilled with seeing the wolf. At the cabin, Maria fixed our last dinner.

"Do you hear that?" Maria stopped on the way to the table with the pasta.

"What? I don't hear anything."

And then I heard it. The wolves, howling in the night. The whole pack. We looked at each other, excited. "Listen. They must be following the migrating caribou herd." We listened to the howling and smiled at each other.

Maria proposed a toast. "To two girls in love having an adventure of a lifetime."

I clinked my plastic mug with hers. "To us."

It's still hard to believe we braved the Alaskan wilderness. Even though, for me, making the trip had been on impulse, it turned out to be a life-changing experience. As I sat there, listening to the voices in the night, I took the gift of the wolf and the gift of Maria's love and placed them deep in my heart. I felt full. We had the wolves, and we had each other. We had only known each other for six weeks, but it seemed as if we had known each other a lifetime. I didn't know that when I met her I would end up following her to the far ends of the earth. But I had, and there we were in a sod-roofed cabin in the middle of the Brooks Range sipping tequila in a rainstorm.

Across the Belly of T.

BY SARAH GROSSMAN

It was resident rotation day at the regional Children's Hospital, and I had been looking forward to it for weeks. We had some difficult patients on rehab, and the doctor who was heading my team was now leaving. He was ineffectual and was even worse with the most difficult patient and her family. A month earlier a 15-year old Native American girl was admitted after becoming a C4 quadriplegic from a car accident.

T. was a beautiful adolescent who now had no movement or sensation below her collarbones. She lay in bed, her black hair splayed against the pillow like a peacock's tail. Her skin was a warm brown, like almonds, smooth and slack against her slight frame, marred only by the tubes coming out of her arm and throat.

Entering T.'s room, one was never certain if one would walk into a dark silence punctuated by the whir, hum, and beeps of machines, or into a space about to erupt, the anger and tension thick as humidity. T. and her mother were prone to fits of rage with screaming, swearing, and objects flying. So far, no one had been able to calm her consistently for more than a day or two at a time. I was hoping the new doctor might be better. All I knew about this doctor was that she was a woman, which would put her a step above the last doctor since T. and her mother seemed to respond better to women than to men.

I was in the silent room, T. feigning sleep as was her morning routine, moving her stockinged feet back and forth. The new doctor
knocked and walked in. I introduced myself and told her that T. was
probably awake. I watched her walk around the side of the bed and
tried to hide my smile as I recognized the exact same eyeglasses that
I wore (when my contacts weren't in) and her down-to-earth style.
I wasn't sure whether or not she might be gay, but I already knew
she was someone I would be interested in getting to know. Dr. Wells
spoke to T., telling her who she was, what she would do for her, and
how she would try to help ease the pain. Her voice was soft and followed the cadence of the machines. She stroked the hair from T.'s
forehead and asked her some questions. I moved to T.'s knee and
bent it up and down, watching their interaction through the corner
of my eye.

T. opened her eyes and looked at the doctor. Dr. Wells asked her
about the dream catcher hanging off her IV pole. T. kept her eyes
open and asked, "You know about that? My mom made it for me."
They talked about dreams while I finished stretching her left leg and
moved to her right. Dr. Wells proceeded with her examination of T.
She gently moved the sheets and gown aside and probed her ab-
domen. Dr. Wells's hands, white and freckled, long fingers softly
pressing and circling T.'s belly, triggered once again T.'s loss for me.
I wanted to give T. my belly with its millions of nerve endings so she
could feel the caring touch of this new person in her life. I wanted
my dreams of T. walking out of her room to get tangled up in her
dream catcher and come true.

Something happened that day in T.'s room, and I thought it was
just for T. Only later would I learn it was for all of us.

Death Talk

BY DEBRA MOSKOWITZ

The first time I approached her, she was sitting naked on the grass by the side of a pond. I believe I had a pair of shorts on. I knew little more than her name and that she was the woman whose lover had died two weeks earlier. Through most of the weekend she had been surrounded by caring friends. This was the first moment I'd seen her alone. Her grief was so fresh it rose like a vapor. It seemed as if her skin would bruise if you brushed against her or laid a comforting hand on her shoulder.

We were at a conference on women and healing at a Boy Scout camp. It was a couple of weeks before the Scouts would arrive, and the camp was filled with women in various states of undress learning about herbs, massage, meditation, and an assortment of alternative healing techniques. The leaves were still young varied hues, not yet settled into the monochromatic green of deep summer. The day was hot, the sky stripped of clouds.

She didn't see me approaching. I called "Hello" a few yards before I reached her, and she looked up and answered without a smile but with a direct and open gaze that she held past the customary duration. I said I was very sorry to hear about Pat, and she nodded and continued to look directly into my face as if she were studying it. I sat down next to her without asking permission, as I would have ordinarily.

Her teenage daughter, who was in the pond with a friend, swam toward the shore like a protective pup coming to check on her mother. She waved her off, saying that everything was okay.

We talked about death, our perceptions and beliefs. We didn't focus on the specific loss she was suffering or loss at all, but about what death is; where we go, what degree of continued contact might be possible. We spoke as if we'd been having such conversations all our lives.

I didn't see her again until about a year later, when I learned that our initial ease was more than a fleeting, grief-induced intimacy. Despite a powerful sexual attraction and emotional rapport, we had difficulty coming together. In the light of the everyday, our difference of age and class and culture appeared insurmountable. We broke up and came back together several times over our first year and a half. But we couldn't manage to stay apart and finally agreed to live together for six months, just to get it out of our systems and move on with our lives.

Now, 20 years after that hot day in June, she still quickens my pulse, and there is no one whose conversation I enjoy more.

I Gave Her a Flower

BY UNCUMBER

She stood up at the end of the film and walked toward the library of The Friends Meeting House, where women were setting out cups for coffee and plates of cookies and cake. There were refreshments during the intermissions of the film benefit for *The New Women's Times*, a feminist newspaper in Rochester, N.Y., previously solvent but now struggling financially, along with many other women's publications in the country in 1983. She wore a maroon sweater that matched the squares in the plaid pattern of her skirt.

It was the way she walked that captured my attention. She strode out of the room with a step that was firm and purposeful, but she moved with a slight sway that indicated ease in her body; a sensuous movement that to this day, 14 years later, makes my heart beat faster and my breath catch in my chest whenever I watch her walk toward or away from me.

I rose immediately and followed her into the next room. As she turned to the bounteous table, I held out my hand and said, "Hello." She accepted my hand, and I slowly told her my name. She looked directly into my eyes and gave her name in return. I confessed to her at a later date that I had given my full name, which is lengthy, at that first meeting because I wanted to keep her hand in mine as long as possible. She confessed that at the time she was wondering how she would remember such a long name and how we could arrange to meet again. Before the films resumed we discovered that we worked in the same large university, and I asked for her office number.

The next day was Saturday. I had arranged to go cross-country skiing with other peace-activist women in a local park. Just as we arrived, a car pulled out of the parking lot. She was driving. I recognized her and waved. She waved back and drove away. One of my friends asked, "Who was that beautiful woman?" I barely heard the question but managed to reply, "I don't really know. I just met her last night."

On Monday I called her and asked to have lunch with her the next day. We agreed to each bring our own sandwiches and meet in the indoor garden of the university hospital. Before going to my office the next morning, I visited a flower shop and looked for just the right blossom for her. A beautiful blue Dutch iris beckoned to me. I carried it carefully through the snow and placed it in a vase on my desk until lunchtime. I brought it to our meeting place. We sat on a bench in the garden and as I handed the flower to her I watched her face closely. I felt excited—hoping she would realize the iris was a symbol of my desire to be closer to her. And I felt frightened— afraid she would find it strange that a woman would bring her a flower and afraid the gesture would put distance between us. To my relief I saw her smile when I handed her the iris. I noticed the color mimicked that of her eyes, which looked directly into mine as she said "Thank you." We ate our lunches. I don't remember what we talked about, but I do remember I walked with her almost the entire way back to her office. It seemed the most natural thing to do to extend the wonderful time with her, as though we had been doing this every day for years.

We talked on the phone and often met for lunch. I didn't know what to do next. I was unable to be more open. I was not sure whether she understood the nature of my attraction to her. I was falling in love, and I was afraid she would be alarmed, repulsed if she came to understand the depth of my feelings. I didn't know if she had any lesbian experience or previous lovers, or if she even knew any lesbians. I was afraid to ask, afraid of losing her. The longer I waited the more I fell in love, and the more afraid I became of doing anything for fear of losing the small bit of contact we had.

She sent me an invitation to her birthday party. It contained a Xerox copy of a photo of her at age one with her cake that held one candle. She was to be 45. I had turned 52 the previous week. Of course I went to the party. After greeting her and meeting some of her friends (all women, a good sign, I thought!), I searched the bookcases and eyed the room decor for clues. Yes! There were volumes of poems by Adrienne Rich on the shelves. There was a unicorn on the wall. My hopes began to rise.

I sat on the floor talking with a few women. She crossed the room to answer the doorbell, and as she passed by me she paused, leaned down slightly, and let her hand rest gently on my hair. I nearly fainted. I lost track of the conversation I was in and only with great effort stammered back to some semblance of coherence. The rest of the evening is a series of scenes in my memory. Watching her talk with friends. Watching her serve food to guests. Watching her open presents. All the while I was trying to keep up a party demeanor.

Toward the end of the evening I felt I had to leave quickly, for I didn't know how I would act if I were left with only a few people present, or if I were the last person to leave. This was not the time to have a serious conversation about the future. Perhaps I could slip quickly past her with a rapid good-bye in a group of people and not be one of those she hugged at the doorway. Was she really ready to hear what I wanted to say? That I wanted to be her lover? That I was in love with her? That I thought we might be happy together for the rest of our lives? And our ages. How would she feel about my being seven years older? How would I dare say all of this? Especially since I was hardly able to keep my balance, hardly able to stay on my feet whenever she came near me.

I dashed for the door as people started leaving. I mumbled that I had to leave. She said, "Wait. Let's make a date for lunch this week. What days are you free?"

"I don't know. I have to go," I stammered.

She followed me to the door and opened her arms to hug me. I literally fell into her embrace, collapsed on her shoulder while my heart, belly, and groin experienced longing and desire in waves such as I had never known before. I buried my face in her neck and moaned, "Oh, no…" I felt that I was embarrassing her and didn't know how to get control of myself and leave. She held me up and gently drew us apart. She was calm and walked with me outside toward my car. I could only murmur, "I must talk with you. I'll call you tomorrow. Will you come?"

She answered, "Yes," and pressed my hand softly.

I left. We did indeed talk the next night. One month later I asked her if she thought we had had enough time to consider all the difficulties we might face if we became lovers, a committed couple. Was she ready and willing to come to bed with me? She said yes, and we began our lives together.

Eleven years ago, three years after that birthday party, I stood one evening at my window and watched as she closed her car door and walked toward my apartment wearing white trousers and a white shirt and carrying a red rose. I said to myself as I felt the familiar excitement rise in me, as that beautiful walking rhythm of hers began moving toward me, "There she is. There's my darling coming home."

At First Sight

BY TZIVIA GOVER

Ask me if I believe in love at first sight, and I will tell you a story. Sure, I'll say. It happened to me; one of those electric moments. The kind you see in movies. When she walked into the room my heart skipped a beat. She laid eyes on me, and I knew I was the girl for her.

Just one glitch. It would take five years before either of us would find out that the other felt the same way.

Here's what happened. It was Super Bowl Sunday, and I was sprawled out across my lover's lap watching the game. She had invited some of her friends—her crowd. We had all played touch football in the street earlier that day. Twice a week we congregated at the two local bars that had "gay night," and on summer weekends we caravaned on motorcycles to local swimming holes. I knew most of her friends by now. But not all. I was about to meet one more.

My eyes were focused on the 50-yard line when the door opened across the room. I didn't recognize the butch who walked in late, just as the first quarter was ending, but everyone else seemed to. She had long hair, the color of clean wood. She was wearing a work shirt, jeans, and loafers without socks. And maybe it was just my imagination, or maybe she really was looking at me like that…

That's when my heart skipped a beat. I didn't dare whisper to my girlfriend, as I normally would have, "Who's that?" for fear something in my tone would give me away.

Yes, this stranger was eyeing me too, I was sure of it. But then I heard her loud, eager voice talking about something quite different. She pushed forward one pierced earlobe in which a diamond stud shone. "Look! We're engaged," she boasted to the room at large. Women scraped themselves up off the couches and carpet where they were sitting to offer congratulations. I stayed put, sinking my head deeper into my girlfriend's chest.

Her name was Whitney. Whit for short. And as it turned out, my girlfriend had a crush on Whitney's girlfriend—her fiancée, I should say. We admitted this to each other as we walked home, drunk, one night several weeks later.

Months passed and the girlfriend and I split up. Irreconcilable similarities. We were both too scared of commitment.

So there I was one night, strolling down Main Street with a buddy I'd known since grade school, and there was Whit, slouching against a corner mailbox as if she were leaning against the bar in some smoky hideaway.

"Hey, there," she said. Her blue eyes locked onto mine, letting me know in a glance that we were the only two people on that crowded street that mattered. Her earlobe was bare. The engagement was off, she told me.

"Too bad," I said, as if I really meant it.

What did we say to each other on that street corner? Neither of us remembers a word until the moment Whit let it slip that she was off to Florida the next week with her new girl. My head was spinning. My heart was skidding to a halt, trying to call itself back. But it was too late. I was smitten. And she was determined. It seemed inevitable we would end up in some complicated triangle.

The triangle was really a sprawling polygon. Whit was collecting lovers like baseball cards that summer. For a few months I let myself be part of her raging geometry lesson.

Timing is everything. In near perfect synchronization, while we were still unhappily involved with each other, Whit met yet another woman, one who wanted all or nothing. And I met a woman too, and this time I demanded all or nothing. We each settled down with our respective someone elses. We started a family. They built a house.

Whit and I ran into one another from time to time at the local dump, at a New Year's Eve party, at a mutual friend's wedding. I tried not to look into her eyes for fear I wouldn't be able to stop. I trusted her about as much as I did the dentist when he says the drill won't hurt.

Timing is everything. Within one month of one another, four years later, Whit and I—sadly, painfully—broke it off with our respective lovers.

When I heard Whit was single again, I vowed to keep my distance. I'd had enough of her geometry lessons. Anyway, I learned mine.

But timing is everything. And one day I was on the beat looking for someone to interview for a newspaper article I was writing about solar energy. Whit, I remembered, as I nearly ran her down with my car (she was jaywalking), had worked installing solar panels on rooftops. I rolled down my window. "Could I ask you a question?"

We met at the curb. We talked solar. She said she could point me in the direction of some sources. I told her I'd call.

"I hate the phone. Can we do this over lunch?" she asked.

I was all reporter at the moment. I had a job to do. She had the information I needed. I consented.

Sometime during that uneasy courtship (during which I kept my senses alert for signs that not all of Whit's oats were thoroughly sown, as she promised they were), she asked if I remembered the first time we met. I wasn't about to admit that I did. So I mentioned the mailbox instead.

"No, it was before that," she insisted. "You were watching the Super Bowl on your girlfriend's lap, and I'd just gotten engaged, and I looked across the room at you…"

So, yeah. I believe in love at first sight. But sometimes what it takes to make it stick is the second sight…or the third.

Lost Decade

My first image was like a flash from an instant camera; I was almost blinded by her electric light and astounded at how everything else dimmed a little.

I had walked into a theater to see a movie with my friend, but instead was met by an undeniable force. She was the assistant manager, and her every word and move captivated me. Auburn hair, endless blue-green eyes, absolutely beautiful and feminine and yet possessing a caustic attitude to be contended with. I had to know her in whatever capacity she would grant me.

I returned the following day, filled out an application, had an interview with the manager, and was hired as a chief of a staff.

The thought of her not being gay never occurred to me, egotistically assuming she was struck by the same powerful surge that wracked me at first glance. But I quickly learned she was in a different place than I was. Although the attraction and discourse was there, so were seemingly insurmountable complications.

She was my boss, forbidden by company policy to date a subordinate. I was 17, and she was 23. Numbers that loomed large in her mind. She was the first woman I had fallen in love with, and she was worried that my adolescent enthusiasm would force her out of a closet she had come to rely on for safety.

But we worked together almost exclusively, becoming very in tune with the other's needs and thoughts. Hours after work were spent over coffee, our professional conversations ebbing away, pulling us into more personal, vulnerable exchanges. Whatever the context of our time together—at work, in cafés, or at one of our homes—I always felt the same intense nervous excitement that sizzled through me since the moment we met.

Little by little she conceded, tried to accept the razor-sharp emotional-intellectual connection we were forging. But she also did everything she could to push it aside. She tested it, fought it, tried to rationalize it away, scared of the ferocity of our acute synchronism.

Eleven months after the first second I saw her, the instant I knew she was the one, she moved away—ostensibly to gather her thoughts, to decide what she wanted, to justify loving me back. The separation was supposed to last only six months, but she became little more than an occasional voice over the phone for a period of 9½ years.

With romantic feelings having been put away, mourned, and ultimately replaced by friendship—the only thing she could offer—we existed on infrequent letters and phone calls, stories of jobs and girlfriends, a quiet denial of our brief, incendiary relationship.

Then she decided to visit. She stepped off the plane and into my arms and hasn't left since. When we saw each other again after nearly a decade, we both realized that what we were denying was the very thing we were searching for in the years lost. Neither of us expected it to happen after so much lost time, but the connection we made at the theater and retained over the miles and years had become stronger, wiser, less volatile than before and with all the complications replaced by acceptance of one another. Our bond now, we saw in each other's eyes, was absolutely vital.

Her move had imperceptibly taken something from both of us, which her return and our subsequent rediscovery of each other replaced, replenished, healed.

I knew she was the love of my life when I caught my first glimpse of her at 17. She was a warm breeze that blew into my heart, a rose that took root and blossomed in my soul. And she remains so.

Cute Meet

BY FAITH JONES

She was my new boss. I can't remember what happened to the old one. I had a student job working on campus at the typesetting service, and they hired a new manager over Christmas break. I came in the first day of the semester and met her. She was a chain-smoking fat woman wearing fatigues. She even wore a khaki combat cap. I found out what a khaki cap was when she opened up one of the machines and tucked her long, dirty-blond hair under the hat so it wouldn't get caught in the works. She carried an odd assortment of stuff in her pockets: tweezers, an X-Acto knife, a pocket calculator. I watched her fix a broken paper feed tray in the big typesetting unit using her tweezers and her teeth. Later she took out the calculator to do an estimate on a job. She could do anything, it seemed.

I was impressed with her, but I didn't really take to her that first day. She was a bit too jolly, too informal. It seemed insincere. She also had an odd habit of quoting bits of poems and song lyrics instead of having conversations. She would respond to something I said with, "Life is real, life is earnest." Or, "Break on through to the other side." I couldn't always tell from the context what these elliptical remarks meant. Old hippie, I thought.

I found out later she didn't take to me either. Thought I was too doctrinaire in my feminism. Middle-class and uppity. A pisher. But I was only 18, so she made allowances.

She had to train me on the new typesetting equipment and while she was at it, she taught me to use the photo-mechanical transfer camera. She seemed to think I was capable. She started telling me stories of her adventures from the '60s. She really was an old hippie, so there were lots of drug stories, but it turned out she also started the first on-campus day care center at our university, even though she didn't have kids herself.

Ultimately I respected her opinion. I told her I was a lesbian as soon as I knew myself. She was OK with it and not surprised like a lot of other people. I appreciated that. Her laugh was so booming you could hear it from outside the building. I used to listen for it as I walked over from the classroom complex to start my work shift.

We lived in the same neighborhood, and she started giving me a lift to school. One semester I was having trouble sleeping. As a result I had trouble getting up. She graciously called me an hour before I was due to be at her house for my ride to campus. Often I was still asleep and she marveled at how long I could talk to her on the phone, carrying on complex conversations, before I actually woke up. She learned to judge from subtle changes in my sleep voice the exact moment when my consciousness emerged.

One time I helped her unpack after moving. Her approach to unpacking was to pour herself a large scotch for each box she emptied. While she was at it she would top off my glass. She gave me the job of putting together the Swedish sofa. I got it right the first try, despite the drinking. She was very impressed. To return the favor she came over and fixed the hinges on my door, which my landlord had been promising to fix for six months. I fell asleep while she was working, and she crept out silently so as not to bother me.

I woke up one morning with a bad cold. The phone rang, and I picked it up but started coughing uncontrollably before I could say hello.

"My God," her voice said in my ear. "All you need is a hankie and a French lover and you'd be *La Bohème*."

This made me laugh, which started the coughing all over again, and I felt a surge of emotion. In the middle of a laughing-coughing fir, and clutching the telephone receiver, I thought, *She is my best friend*. Which was weird because she was my boss and almost 20 years my senior.

We never talked about her sexuality until two years after we met. Something depressing was happening at work, so we were spending the evening systematically getting drunk together. We had already drunk a bottle of tequila. Walking from my house to hers in search of another bottle, I asked her out of the blue, "Are you a lesbian?"

And she replied, "Not yet."

Later on that night, she was.

Faith Jones and Winnifred Tovey have lived together for 11 years.

In a Crowded Room

BY LISA ORTA

It was February 3, 1987. I was sitting in my car at the Fort Mason parking lot in San Francisco, cursing the half-baked idea that I would meet someone if I just did the things I enjoyed doing. I can still hear what was running through my head on that cold, lonely night: *Great. This is just great. I'll go in, stand in line with all these straight people, sit down, watch the play, feel awkward during intermission, and drive home alone. Why should this night be different from the last three?* There was no answer in the Haggadah to that one.

My best friend had died from AIDS complications in November of 1982, and I was relatively single since then. I knew it was time to come out of my shell, but the dating I had done through the personal ads was remarkably less than satisfying. One things I love to do is to go to plays, especially experimental theater. So I bought season tickets to the Magic Theater, conscious of the fact that if I bought tickets with a friend I wouldn't cruise the crowd as effectively. The Magic is not a gay theater; I was being a purist. The woman I was prepared to meet would have to comfortable in a straight environment, a literary and artistic environment. And she would have to be comfortable enough in her lesbian identity to exude it both blatantly and subtly in order to attract attention and interest. I was confident I could take it from there.

Waiting in the will call line, feeling awkward and conspicuous, I heard someone call my name. I looked up and around to see a former coworker, Irene, with her partner, Charlotte. And there she was with them. Tall, piercing green eyes, seductive smile, kind and gentle.

"Are you here by yourself?" asked Irene.

I nodded, relieved, excited, nervous. I knew at that moment I was no longer by myself.

"This is our friend, Karen," said Irene.

Quick on the draw, Charlotte manipulated our seating assignments so that Karen and I ended up sitting next to each other, our legs touching but not touching. All I remember of the first act is the sound of my heart beating faster and louder as I plotted my intermission moves. Then, in the blink of an eye it was intermission, and Karen was gone. I jumped over Charlotte and Irene, chasing after Karen through the crowded aisles. After some pretty aggressive crowd behavior, I found Karen smoking in the stairwell. To my dismay she thwarted my attempts at conversation and turned away from me repeatedly to exhale. The evening did not have a satisfactory ending. I drove away alone, confused, rejected.

The following Saturday I was retrieving my clothes from the dry cleaner's, and again I heard Irene call my name. Charlotte pulled their green Honda over and double-parked on Market Street. Irene jumped out of the passenger side and asked in her signature loud and direct manner, "So, Lisa, which do you prefer? Men or women?"

"Women," I responded, clueless about the meaning of this line of questioning.

"Well, Karen thought you were straight. So I told her I'd ask you. I was pretty sure you liked women, but I guess you can never be sure."

We both had a good laugh, and Irene took my phone number. We planned to have dinner together before the next play, which was coming up the next weekend. One mystery solved.

All I remember about the second meeting was our legs deliberately touching under the table. Charlotte and Irene mercifully chose a crowded pizzeria. I don't remember eating. I don't remember any part of the conversation. And I don't remember the play. I just remember a sensation of warmth and joy and intimacy. There wasn't that old familiar feeling of desperation or manipulation or the need to impress. I was purely and simply myself with Karen. I had been alone for so long that it seemed my character was stripped bare; with her it could be rebuilt upon its own foundation. I knew this time things could go slowly, at least by lesbian standards. We dated for six weeks before sleeping together, for several months before moving in together, and lived together for four years before having our first child.

Ten years later our relationship has weathered many twists and turns. We are as entwined as any conventional heterosexual couple—we own our own house, cars, have two kids, and are expected as each other's work-related social functions. Our opposite families treat us as in-laws, and we are comfortable in our neighborhood and community. That electric spark ignited ten years ago may have worn to a more even glow, but we have found what we were both looking for back then—the space to be self-defined in a relationship that is constant, supportive, and loving.

Sunshine Day

BY HARLYN AIZLEY

To brighten up a cold day in January of 1993, a friend dared my sister to audition for the touring company of *The Real Live Brady Bunch*. Two days later my sister was recruited to play "Jan." Two weeks later she quit her job, sold her stuff, and started rehearsals in Providence, R.I. Two weeks after that she called me.

"Come to the opening, and make sure you say hi to Faith. She's the girl at the piano."

"Why?"

"Because I think you'll like her."

"Because she's gay?"

"Because I think you'll like her."

"What does she look like?"

"I'll send you a picture."

In the mail arrived a press kit with photographs from *People* magazine, the *Chicago Tribune*, and the *L.A. Weekly*. This girl was famous. And in a month she was leaving the tour and moving to San Francisco.

As for me, my brain was busily preoccupied with whether or not to enter medical school in Boston in two months. My heart, having thought this dilemma quite ridiculous from the start (Me? Cut up a dead person?), was in desperate need of a break. I took my night off and went to the show. Afterward, in feigned nonchalance, I ambled up to the brown-eyed girl at the piano and said, "My sister said to say hello."

One week later, as Boston was being buried under another two feet of snow, the Bradys moved on to San Francisco for a six-week stay. My sister called again.

"Faith says she has a crush on you."

"Come on, we just said hi."

"Come to San Francisco…soon."

With my brain now preoccupied with which computer could best handle the anatomy program it was suggested we buy before classes started, my heart sneaked away and bought a ticket to San Francisco.

In San Francisco Faith and I were afraid to talk to each other. We went to restaurants and parties and strolled up and down the hills, always making sure we were accompanied by at least three other Bradys. At last one morning, when "Marsh," my sister, and I were supposed to meet Faith at her new apartment, I noticed I was the only one prepared to leave. "Marcia" and "Jan" sat determinedly in their small hotel beds.

"Go ahead," they directed. So I did.

Faith and I went for coffee in the Mission. We wandered up to Noe Valley, and then decided to drive over to the Golden Gate Park. I thought she was amazing, interesting, and so beautiful and sweet. So as we drove past the University of San Francisco Medical School, I felt safe enough to confess that I had applied there but was rejected.

Faith responded, "Sometimes things just aren't meant to be."

Alas. I knew she was referring to us. My heart joined my brain and took refuge in the 150 years of school ahead of me. There would be no time for romance.

That night at the theater, my sister grabbed me by the arm and dragged me into her dressing room.

"She likes you."

"No, she doesn't. She said things aren't meant to be."

"You're an idiot."

"Thanks."

The next day I went to see a psychic. The psychic lived in a house by the ocean. She told me she didn't see a relationship in my near future. I paid her $80 and went to meet my sister and Faith for dinner.

I was brooding over the bad news when my sister got up and went to the bathroom, leaving Faith and me alone again. We sat in silence. I assumed she was merely tolerating my presence, just biding her time until "Marcia's" or "Peter's" gay sister arrived the following week, when she suddenly winked at me. At least it looked like a wink. But it could have been a tic. I figured she was probably thinking, *Shit, I winked.* I decided to help her out and pretended I didn't notice.

Later that evening we went to a show. Faith sat down on one side of me and "Jan," my sister, on the other. Somewhere in the middle, before intermission, I felt a soft hand on my neck. Hoping to God it wasn't my sister, I turned first to Faith and thankfully saw a smile. Later that night, as Faith and I sat alone together watching the stars in Buena Vista Park, she asked if I knew how much she liked me.

"No," I said.

"You're an idiot," she said.

The next day we raced off to a cabin on the Russian River, where I contemplated calling in sick to extend my weeklong vacation. But in honor of my heart, which was back on the scene, and the magic Faith and I slowly were finding between us, I decided to tell the truth. I called in "in love" and said I would be gone for another five days.

Encouraged, my heart now was hollering, drowning out my brain and all of its worries. I deferred medical school for a year. Faith and

I spent that year (and more) commuting back and forth between Boston and San Francisco and later Los Angeles, where she moved to work on another show.

Before we met both Faith and I had been struggling with the confusing realization that success was leading us away from rather than toward our truest dreams. I think it was surviving the challenge of a long-distance relationship and two very separate worlds that enabled each of us ultimately to challenge ourselves. With a year I decided to withdraw entirely from medical school to pursue writing, my first love. Faith opted out of the world of television and moved east to pursue a career in music.

When Faith moved east we moved in together; not at all in the fashion my brain had planned I eventually would live with someone. We were only together a year and a half, we never lived in the same city, neither of us had jobs, and we were moving into a one-bedroom apartment. But it was hearts rule now. We held our breath and jumped.

Ever since that leap we have found in each other both our muse and our stability. Four and a half years later, we continue to follow our dreams, independently and together.

Faith likes to tell the story of how she finally had to accost me in a theater to get me to believe she liked me. My sister, no longer Jan Brady, likes to remind us that we owe her one.

Blueprints

BY THERESA CARILLI

Six months later, on Valentine's Day during a blizzard, I stopped by un-expectedly with some flowers and chocolates. She had just started a fire in the fireplace. Tearfully she proclaimed her love for me, and I returned the proclamation. It would have been perfect had we not been involved with other lovers.

Jane and I have been together for almost eight years, depending on when we date our relationship. We met eight years ago, but we first got together six months afterwards. This becomes particularly special for both of us since we are not the type to court someone for six months. Meet. Date. Attraction. Sleep together. Relationship? Maybe. Maybe not. But truly I think our six-month courtship made us sure of our connection.

We work at a small Midwestern university. A year before meeting her, I finally finished my dissertation and took a one-year appoint-ment at the university. Meanwhile, Jane, the women's studies coor-dinator at the time, was on sabbatical in San Francisco. My col-leagues kept telling me I would "really like Jane" and that she and I "had a lot in common." At the first women's studies meeting I at-tended, I found myself arguing with one of Jane's male colleagues, who was proposing a course examining American literature from a feminist perspective. The course would examine the works of Hem-ingway, Fitzgerald, and the like and would have been team-taught with Jane. Though I was not yet a regular faculty member and had never met Jane, I argued vehemently that she would not be in favor of such a course. I don't know what compelled me to argue so strongly on her behalf.

At the beginning of the next year, I was hired at the university and attended the first women's studies meeting of the semester where I met Jane for the first time. The meeting was held in our cafeteria/lounge area. I was trying to be in touch with my feminine side and wore a skirt to the meeting, which made me rather irritable. Jane entered the cafeteria to meet the committee members. She greeted us by telling us that her luggage from San Francisco was lost and she would be wearing the same outfit for the next several days. I liked her immediately. She was so genuine and honest. I noticed her strong nose, gorgeous blue eyes, and magnificent carriage.

As she was introduced to me, we made eye contact, and I told her I had lived in San Francisco for awhile. Somehow, and I'm not sure how, we suddenly got into a heated discussion about Spike Lee's movie *Do the Right Thing*. I learned that Jane's area of expertise was African-American literature, and I argued with her about the depiction of Italian-Americans in the movie. I argued as though I were speaking to Spike Lee himself. I'm sure she thought I was just plain nuts or had a chip on my shoulder, but, supportively, she listened to my diatribe. The damage was already done. We were either going to be lovers or enemies. My track record in the Midwest had led to me to expect the latter.

The following week, at a women's studies brown-bag event (which means bring your lunch and listen to a speaker), Jane, now clothed in a tasteful suit, introduced the speaker and sat down to eat her lunch—cottage cheese and vegetables. As the speaker began to talk, she accidentally spilled her entire container of cottage cheese all over herself. I fell madly in love with her.

Later that week I invited her into my office under the pretense of discussing literature. By casually talking about our lovers, we came out to one another and began a friendship. Both of our lovers were in other states, and neither of us were in very good relationships. Next came weekly dinners where we talked about our lives and dreams. We had such incredible rapport and all too often I would think to myself, *if only…*

Six months later, on Valentine's Day during a blizzard, I stopped by unexpectedly with some flowers and chocolates. She had just started a fire in the fireplace. Tearfully she proclaimed her love fore me, and I returned the proclamation. It would have been perfect had we not been involved with other lovers.

"I wanted to get you a card," she said. "But I couldn't find one that expressed my feelings."

We discussed the possibility of just having an affair. How silly of us. We had a magical connection and were guided to one another by some inexplicable force. Sometimes I believe individuals can see their future reflected in their lover's eyes. In those few moments of recognition, we see a blueprint of our lives intertwined together.

Slowly, painfully, and carefully, we broke it off with our lovers. I can go on endlessly about Jane's wonderful personality traits, her grace and beauty, and how crazy I am about her, but for me, it all comes down to this: Jane makes me laugh, and she makes me laugh at myself. She still listens attentively to my diatribes, but now at least I can pause in the middle and listen to how ridiculous I might sound.

Bridging the Gulf

BY SUSAN LEE SILLS

The word was out from the university administration building:
The feuding between computer science and electrical engineering
had to stop. Since dealing with faculty is described as "herding cats,"
it was decided the staff would be the ones tapped to promote this
new policy of friendliness.

I was the new "acting" manager of electrical engineering; Judy
was the well-established manager of computer science. I was almost
at the end of a self-imposed year of healing after the breakup of my
first relationship, newly returned to the university, in the closet
(until I was off new-hire probation), and with no idea how to meet
women. Judy was dating a couple of women, also in the closet at
work, the mother of two teenage boys, and definitely not looking for
someone.

It was December; the announcements had just come out inviting
people to apply to attend a big university-wide conference for department managers in San Francisco. And the person coordinating
the response from campus was…Judy! So rather than simply send
the form over to her office—we were in adjoining buildings, separated by a vast academic gulf—I decided to just walk over and work
on being friendly with computer science. What a concept!

Walking into the reception area, I handed the application form
to the young woman at the front desk and looked around. Fate truly
works wonders. Judy's door was open, she didn't have anyone with

her, and she wasn't on the phone. She looked up (briefly), smiled, and went back to work. I almost lost it right then. I remember thinking to myself: "Wow, is she hot!"

Managing to babble something to the receptionist, I stood there as long as I could, looking at Judy and trying to pretend I was having a conversation. It must have appeared pretty strange. Finally I couldn't think of any more reasons to hang out so I went back to my office.

Unbeknownst to me, Judy then came out of her office and asked, "Who was that and what on earth did she want?" Which shows that at least I made an impact, even if not exactly the one I might have wanted. She later described me as conspicuously gawking.

I had no idea if Judy was a lesbian, if she was single, if she dated, nothing. And worse yet, I had no idea how to find out! But food is a great breaker of ice. I decided to ask her to lunch, be friendly, and try somehow to find out what I needed to know.

After some slow starts we finally set up a time for lunch at a Thai place near campus. I was tremendously nervous, and Judy wondered why I seemed so keyed-up. We sat down and ordered, then chatted about all the things one finds out about work colleagues. She had two sons, was divorced, had worked for the university for two years. I told her I was divorced, that I had worked at the university for a number of years, left, and came back a few months ago, and really needed her help with bridging the gulf between our departments and with my underdeveloped skills as a manager. She seemed pleased and flattered by that.

Then she asked me, "Do you have a roommate?"

Looking deeply into her glorious brown eyes, I replied softly, "No." Then I jumped. "Yes! I do, yes. I have a roommate."

Alas, I had managed to totally forget the young woman who was my fiscal, but not physical, roommate, and I was mortified to realize it. Judy grinned. She later said that she knew right then I was a lesbian because my confusion was revealing. If only I had been as sure of her at that time, I would have saved myself a great deal of anxiety.

It took me until the actual conference to get up enough nerve to officially come out to her. And to find out that she was a lesbian too.

Eight Ball in the Corner Pocket

BY BETTY JO MOORE

It was 1976. I was a single, free-as-the-wind, 42-year-old butch traveling from Texas to Arkansas on vacation. The relationships I had had before were short-lived. I couldn't seem to find that one person I wanted to have with me for the rest of my life.

When I arrived in Tulsa, Okla., I decided to spend the night and check out the bars. In the first bar two women were playing pool. I ordered a beer and put up my quarter to challenge the game. Each of the women introduced herself. Marian had a quick smile and a sporty look about her, which attracted me at once.

Marian lost the pool game, and I started playing with June. Marian carried on a conversation with me as we played. It was the usual what-kind-of-work-do-you-do conversation. She was in recreation and I was in physical education. One plus!

Suddenly she said she had to go. It was my shot, so I took quick aim at the eight ball and planted it in the side pocket. I said, "Darn it, June, you win," and caught Marian before she reached the door.

I asked her out to eat with me, pleading that I was a stranger in town. We went to the Pizza Hut and, looking at her across the table, I felt as if I had known her all my life. While we were eating she commented that she felt the same way.

I can't say it was love at first sight, but maybe second.

Although she said she didn't do such things, I talked her into going to my motel with me. We didn't get any sleep and knew a great deal about each other by the time the sun rose. It was a beautiful night.

As the time drew close for me to leave, she seemed scared to death, but later told me she was fantasizing about going off to Texas with this person.

I left Tulsa and went on to visit my friends in Arkansas. I wrote Marian letters and mailed them at truck stops on the way. I was supposed to stay a week with my friends, but after three days I told them I had to go back to Tulsa.

When I saw Marian again I knew it was love. She was frightened to death and told me I could come into her apartment if I promised not to touch her. She was nervous and told me to have a nice trip back to Texas. I started my drive back. I wrote her letters and mailed them. I told her I wanted her to come to Texas because I had fallen in love with her.

I stopped off for two days at some relatives' house in Dallas, then continued my trip home, still writing Marian letters all the way.

When I opened the door to my apartment the phone was ringing. I grabbed the receiver and heard, "Betty, I quit my job, and I'm coming to Texas."

I told her I would meet her at a bar in Austin, and then she could follow me home. We spent the night at a motel in Austin and caravaned home the next day.

We were each like a shoe that had finally found its mate: at ease, warm and comfortable from the beginning. Our deep love continues toward the 22nd year.

Mi Amor

BY SUE PIESER

The first Sunday in February of 1996 was the evening I met the great love of my life. At that time I didn't go out to clubs much. When other volunteer English as a Second Language teachers wanted to meet at The Easy, one of the local lesbian clubs, for a Latino drag show, I decided to join them. The idea of meeting a girlfriend at a male drag show was not even remotely tucked away in the deep recesses of my mind.

Although I am usually running late, on this particular evening I was early. I walked into the bar to be greeted by a menagerie of beautiful drag queens and many gay men. The women were few and far between. I found a nice comfortable spot to relax against the back wall. Here I had a chance to watch the parade of people whooshing past me. Everyone seemed friendly. They smiled at me, but nobody talked to me. I knew that I was welcome there, yet I was nervous because I was alone and one of the few gringas there that night. I kept an eye on the door for my coworker, Martha. Finally it dawned on me that I needed to accept the fact that no one was coming. I was at the bar alone.

I bought another beer and settled into my spot. There were two men sitting next to me, and a beautiful woman sat next to them. She was wearing a dark, silky blazer and white turtleneck. Her hair was reddish-brown, shoulder-length, and curly. I wanted to talk to her, but I felt shy and out of practice. She seemed so confident and easy with her friends. I liked the way she laughed with them. I didn't want to catch her eye, so I just stole looks in her direction. I decided the best approach was to talk to her friends. I wanted them to be our intermediaries. The were kind, but shy, so my plan didn't work.

When I returned from another trip to the bar, I was greeted by an incredible sight. Standing in the exact spot I had inhabited stood the woman. Uh-oh, what should I do? There wasn't many places to stand, and I thought I needed to find another spot. This had to be a coincidence. She could not have known I was standing there. She flashed a smile at me as I started to walk away. Then she lightly grabbed my arm and said coyly, "I was just saving our spot." Her rich Mexican accent melted my heart immediately.

I couldn't blow my chance for a good retort. "Actually you look great there. I don't think you should move. I'm fine where I am."

I didn't even feel nervous as we chatted. It was kind of easy. She told me that her name was Blanca, and she was from Mexico. I told her I was waiting for the other teachers who, at this point, I was convinced weren't going to show. She knew most of the drag queens who passed us. We were laughing like old friends when Martha finally walked into the room.

Martha was impressed that I had made a friend so quickly. She and I had never asked discussed my sexual orientation, but before the end of the night she would have crystal-clear proof that I was partial to women. We all danced together, but Martha conveniently took breaks, which gave me a chance to dance alone with Blanca. When she touched my back or looked into my eyes I felt eager with anticipation. I had no idea that she was the woman with whom I would spend my life, but I was intensely attracted to her energy, the way she carried herself, and the way she looked.

Even though she was acting sweet to me and buying me drinks, I still didn't feel sure she was interested in me. I thought she was just a gracious woman, perhaps amusing herself with my company for the evening. She asked me if I had a girlfriend…or a boyfriend. I told her I was single, and she seemed amazed.

"How could someone as wonderful as you be single? That couldn't be possible," she said warmly, melting my heart.

When I asked about her living situation, she said she had broken up with her girlfriend three weeks prior to that evening.

Giddy with dancing, drinking, and socializing, I decided to come out to Martha. "It's too bad that she just broke up with her girlfriend," I told Martha in private. "She is just so damn cute."

Well, Martha was keeping an eye on how things were going. She looked me straight in the eye and said, "It's quite obvious that she likes you."

That confirmation somehow made all abstract things in my mind very concrete. I was telling Martha that I felt like Blanca felt as if the world was her candy store now that she was a single woman; that it was hard for me to trust that this was really about me. Martha just laughed and said that Blanca had chosen a sweet piece of candy. I tried to let my insecurities take a vacation for the evening so that I could continue to have fun. We were attracted to each other, that was obvious, but I didn't know how that was going to play itself out. However, in the meantime, I relished the attention.

We watched the drag queens perform, then we continued dancing when they took breaks. In the custom so typical of her Latina nature, Blanca asked me, "Will you have a shot of tequila with me?"

I protested mildly, saying I really shouldn't. She went on to describe how warm I would feel inside and how it would be good for me to appreciate Mexican culture, and, lo and behold, I ended up saying yes. We walked to the bar and she ordered one shot and a beer. I asked her where her shot was, and she said she didn't drink tequila. We laughed.

In fact, we spent a lot of time that evening laughing. We laughed after our fist kiss on an overstuffed chair next to the bar, and we laughed in the car on the way to my apartment. I felt so much more intoxicated by her company than by the alcohol, and I didn't want the evening to end.

Now it is almost a year and a half later, and we are planning to have our first child together. I'm glad that first night never ended.

First Encounter/First Contact

BY RAVEN SPRING

FIRST ENCOUNTER

I was 38 years old and walking by a yucca plant in Santa Fe, N.M., the day I realized I was a lesbian. It was right before Christmas, and the sky was pale blue. It happened between one step and the next. As the cosmos heard me breathe those words in a gasp of exultation and wonder, she perked up her starry ears and said, "Ah, now she is ready!" Two weeks later my world shifted forever.

I was in the process of deciding where to move to next: Eugene, Ore., or Seattle. It was January of 1995. Out of the pale blue sky fell a letter from an old friend whom I hadn't spoken to for 17 years, and who coincidentally (?) lived in the Seattle area. I immediately called her in great excitement, and while speaking with her remembered that she was the first lesbian I had ever knowingly met.

I was 21 at the time, and we were going to school together in Detroit. One afternoon we were sitting in my apartment, she in the armchair, I across from her on the couch, and she just blurted out the L word. *Lesbian.* She said she was a lesbian. I was young, a white upper-class suburbanite from outside of Boston. I had only read the word maybe twice in my life and likened those people to Moonies: just plain nuts and dangerous. My heart met my tonsils while I tried surreptitiously to press my bulging eyeballs back into their diminished sockets. "Oh," is all I remember saying. That was my first up close and personal meeting with that alien life form. And now I was one of them.

I chuckled at the fates as I wound up my telephone conversation with my old friend. During the brief catching up, I asked C. if she knew anyone in the counseling arena in the Seattle area. I had a degree and no job to attach it to. She gave me the name of an ex-girlfriend and said she would also pass my name on to her.

Two days later I received a message on my machine. "I like your message (wolves howling)," the caller said. "When's a good time to talk?" I called back and left her a message: "Friday after 6 P.M." And so our first "date" was set, although I doubt either of us knew it by that name at the time.

To fully appreciate our first conversation, I have to remind you, the readers, as well as myself that this was a total stranger on the other end of the line who lived 2,000 miles away. We talked for hours—about what, I couldn't tell you, but it wasn't all about job opportunities. Thinking back on those first hours, it was if we had picked up on a conversation we had started about 2,000 years ago. It all seemed so familiar: her voice, her manner, her story, our voice, our manner, our story. Something ancient, primeval, cellular. She was an old friend I had misplaced, forgotten, meant to call all these years. She was a piece of me that I had packed away in my mother's attic. I felt like she already knew me. I didn't have to explain. But I was also afraid. Afraid that I would suddenly be caught by some chance word or sound. That by the sheer familiarity between us I would be lured into a false sense of trust and would become suddenly the brunt of some joke. I wavered between that sense of familiarity and a sense of fearful distrust. When would that remark come that would separate me once again from that sacred part of myself? It never did.

Our first encounter was voice to voice, but in that meeting our souls clasped hands and held each other in a glad embrace of re-union. First encounter.

FIRST CONTACT

As the hours flowed into days and weeks, and J.'s voice became a part of my cells, I realized that I was falling in love, or recognizing a love I had known ages before. I wondered how I could feel such a strong bond with someone I had never seen or touched further than a photograph. One day I heard myself say, "I love you." Aghast that I had left myself wide open for the inevitable embarrassed silence that was sure to follow as she tried to think of how to graciously say she felt nothing, I raced on, trying to cover my tracks. But instead of camouflaging my true feelings and turning to the weather, I heard my voice saying, "Marry me!" *Oh, God,* I screamed to myself. *Surely you have gone too far.*

She said, "Yes!"

It was now time to see each other face to face. After discussing this date or that, it was finally settled. On February the seventeenth, I would meet J. at the Albuquerque International Airport, baggage claim area, outside. I could hardly remember how to breathe that whole day. I was in an altered state of petrified joy. Finally I would see the disembodied voice come through those sweet lips. I drove to the airport and parked myself at the baggage claim, daring anyone to try to get me to budge. I sat in the car. I stood outside the car. I paced around the car. I breathed. I glared at the sliding doors every time they slid open to see if they might reveal my love, my self. Minutes turned over and over. I wanted to scream, "Where are you?"

Suddenly out of the dark from behind a pillar came her voice. "It's me," she called.

She had been spying on my rituals of impatient searching. I felt naked, vulnerable. As I put on my "brave" smile, I could feel my solar plexus shuddering and my heart pounding hope. She came close to me, and I recognized her in all ways. I encircled her in my arms, and I kissed my sweet love long and passionately on the lips. First contact.

J. and I married each other the next evening up in the mountains of New Mexico. Our witnesses were the blood-red wedding rock we found in the hills earlier that day, the scent of incense, a candle of passion, and the hot steamy waters of the tubs we bathed each other in. I moved to Seattle six weeks later, into my new hearth, and have been here loving and growing with my wife ever since.

Are We There Yet?

BY JUDITH K. WITHEROW

Not long ago I was sitting on the front steps thinking about life. The porch had chairs and a swing, but I'm always more comfortable when the earth is at eye level. My partner, Sue, was watering the yard and doing basic weed, seed, and feed stuff while I observed each movement her body made.

As a random thought I asked her if the neighbors imagined we were queer. I knew the answer seconds before her tongue and brain formed the reply. The spirits know I've seen the writing on the eyes throughout my lifetime. Experience has also taught me that any sentence beginning with a high-pitched "Judith!" will not be good.

While contemplating a reply she ran her dirt-covered hand through her short hair. "Judith, think about it. Two women have lived in the same house for the past 16 years. Nothing but women's meetings and parties take place here. Neither woman is ever seen dating a man. Do you honestly believe the neighbors think one is a lesbian, and the other one is her straight friend? Wait a second…you think because you wear your hair in a long braid and have three kids the neighbors assume you're hetero? Admit it."

Admit it. I don't think so. How could she be so dead-on, mind-reading accurate? It had to be more than 20 years of living and loving together. Could she have developed my ability to suspend belief and spider-spin fantasy?

Fantasy. What a feather-soft word. It can erase or add any event to my life with a mere thought. Didn't it inspire the "want to" in me long before we met? Sue was always my lover. When she was first introduced to me, I wanted to say, "We've already met." But I didn't. I remember being very articulate and restrained. That was some other Judith babbling on about the weather. The same athletic woman who managed to drop a beer on her foot. That woman was pathetic.

It was hard to avoid being smug when reality and fantasy blended so perfectly. Curly, wild hair. Hair that would have made Janis Joplin's look as straight as mine. Tough. Sue taught self-defense and rode a huge motorcycle. When that other Judith mentioned something about having a small Honda, the room turned soundproof waiting for the punch line. It was the perfect moment for her to adjust her breasts and steer the conversation in a totally different direction.

There were so many things I instantly loved about Sue. So many they couldn't be put into spoken words. I didn't want to scare her away by saying how perfect I thought she was. If she knew, perhaps she would think she deserved someone better than me. If I had seen beyond my fantasy, I would have known that Sue was not exactly the same as her outward image.

The time was the mid '70s. During that period everyone was "dressing down," Sue included. In my mind I thought it was amazing that so many poor women were also dykes. Later on I discovered this was intentional. It had something to do with being secure about yourself. Wouldn't you know? I was finally able to afford clothes that someone else hadn't half worn out, but the rules had changed.

We were submerged in different aspects of the lesbian-feminist movement. Sue, although six years younger, had more years of activism. I thought she was from my class background, but the exact opposite was true. This was discovered later, and later, as usual, was too late. Race, class, and culture were things I wanted completely understood. She was too important to play games with. My life was hers—my real life—if she wanted it.

If there were any books on lesbian courtship, they must have been kept in a back room. My fantasy evolved from magazines, music, and movies. After a lifetime of hardship, I wanted someone strong to lean on. But I wasn't sure how or if role-playing figured in attracting this dyke of my dreams.

There was a deep need within me to make her proud. To impress her I took her to a turkey shoot. Yes, a turkey shoot. You shoot at bull's-eye targets with a .12 gauge shotgun. I shot against 19 men and was the winner. The prize was a frozen turkey. It didn't occur to me that guns might not be part of her culture. I was too busy strutting around to notice her reaction. A number of guys were pissed at losing and tried their best to figure a way to discount my center shot. When it was settled Sue grabbed and hugged me. She thought besting so many was great.

Shopping for her birthday that first year is another memory that confounds me. When I was growing up, you were lucky if someone even remembered the date. There were no presents or cake. Generations of poverty taught you to just be glad you survived another year.

What gift do you buy for a T-shirt- and ripped-jeans-wearing kind of woman? You take your money, love, and lust and head for one of those swank stores. Yeah. Some flimsy, frilly, see-through night thing you've seen pictured in some catalog. *Judith?* a small voice inside my head inquired of me. *Do you recall Sue wearing anything when she goes to bed?* What? I was distracted with my shopping. Did someone say something?

There it was. A girlie gown in some unknown shade of green. Fuzzy stuff was all around the neck and bottom of it. The matching panties had less than enough material to cover her crotch. You go, girl! This outfit beat a turkey shoot all the way to hell and half the Appalachians.

Everything went fine until I went to the counter to pay. The clerk asked if I was buying it for myself. I should have said yes. Instead I blushed and mumbled something about a present for my sister. The reply got me the look the other Judith deserved. Your sister? Geez, Judith, and you were doing so fine in this alien atmosphere.

Looking back over the past 20 years never fails to make me laugh or sigh. How can one woman be so lucky? I am so well-loved that the word *monogamy* is the better part of me.

I'm still looking for that book of dyke definitions. Sue is right when she says that *butch* and *femme* are only words. We each have our own strengths and weaknesses, our own likes and dislikes. This doesn't explain her desire to always put on femme costumes for every occasion. I'm just thankful that gene was passed on to one of my brothers, leaving me to choose between jeans or a tux.

The neighbors probably do think we're a queer couple. If they have a problem with our lifestyle, they also have enough sense to keep it to themselves. Sue thinks she's the realistic one, but I'm the one they have yet to see prancing around in a dress.

I watch as the clouds begin to darken and curdle around the treetops. The rain will soon put an end to her yard work and my backward journey. What would she think if I joined her in the newly-mulched flower bed? The softness and scent of the shredded pine have my thoughts racing. What if….

Fantasy, thy name is Sue.

Part II
She Said, She Said

Whacked With a 2-by-4

BY MARGARET "RABBITT" LORING

I wasn't looking for love when my sweetie found me; I was helping friends raise a roof. Not a wild party, mind you, but literally putting the roof on their house.

I met Jackson there, along with a lot of other wimmin, and didn't pay any particular attention to her as we did different jobs during the day. When it came time to lay the plywood, we became a ground team. We passed up the sheets; they marked them and passed them back down; we cut them and passed them back up. The problem was with the cutting. Jackson held while I cut, but the chips flew into my eyes. We couldn't find any goggles.

"Here," she said, removing her glasses. "Try these."

I put them on and tried to see the line on the plywood. The board looked two-dimensional, flat but wavy at the same time. It made my head feel suddenly inflated.

"How do you see through these?" I asked, handing them back. As I stretched my arm toward her, I looked into her eyes and saw her for the first time. Those eyes, green as a moss-covered log, the most beautiful I had ever seen, struck to the core of my heart.

"Hello!" I said, as though we had just been introduced. Then I saw fine, dark hair falling to her waist from under a black Bugs Bunny cap; a neon smile of pure white teeth, one broken at a rakishly sexy angle; fingers, fine and sensitive, that had seen as much of life as my own. It suddenly occurred to me that she might have been flirting with me all along—the looks, the sexy insinuations, telling me to get the pencil myself out of her breast pocket.

Later, around the fire, I asked our hosts if they had any idea about building a deck for a hot tub—my next project. Jackson slipped me her number on a small piece of paper and said she would help.

"You'd come all the way from El Paso?" I asked. It was an hour away, and I couldn't imagine why she would want to drive so far.

"Yes," she said with such a smile I should have been knocked off my feet right then and there. But, no. I needed to be whacked in the head with a 2-by-4.

I saw Jackson the following week at a concert, which reminded me that I needed to set a date for the deck building. The friend I was with told me to invite her to join us, then sat strategically so that I would be between the two of them. During the concert I kept finding my arm on the back of Jackson's chair and my knee inching closer to hers. I thought I should act like I was "with" the womyn I came with, but I kept wondering why I felt so attracted to Jackson.

A few days later Jackson came over to help with the deck. I finally "got it" enough to decline other offers of help, and it was just the two of us. She walked into the house and noticed a picture on my wall.

"So who's the Baha'i?" she asked.

She shared my obscure religion! My heart leaped. Not only was there another lesbian Baha'i in the world, but one who was interested in me! I began to think this could develop into something serious.

It has. She came back the next day and suddenly the 50 miles between us was no impediment. We have not been parted since.

I Didn't Want to Go

BY RHONDA JACKSON

I didn't want to go. A ringing telephone on Saturday morning is usually my mom checking up on me. This time it was my ex-girlfriend. Two dykes needed help raising a roof on the house they were building. My ex was cooking. I said no. I had a thesis to write.

After hanging up the phone I had second thoughts. It was a constructive way to procrastinate. I hated writing my thesis. The food would be good...and free. And I might meet someone there. That was the key. I called back and said I would be there with my hammer and healthy appetite.

I called my friend Mary, who didn't want to go. She said to look for a woman with class (meaning power tools and a graduate degree) for her. Anybody like that is rare and a keeper. I didn't make any promises.

As it turned out I was the first one there. Gradually other women began arriving. A 1965 Galaxie drove up. Red with a white top. Promising. Two women got out. Oh, well.

We got started on the work. I'm afraid of heights but tried to work on the roof anyway. I got stuck, and they had to carry me back to safety. So far I wasn't making a good impression on any of these women, I could tell. It was mortifying. There were kids all over, dangling from the rafters, and I couldn't climb over two feet without freezing up.

I shied away from my ex-girlfriend. I wasn't sure of what she wanted, which is why I had ended the relationship. I still wasn't sure. In moving out of range, I bumped into a ladder. A nice-looking woman was on it giving directions to her son about nailing supports. I liked the way she worked with him. The owner of the house and work foreman introduced us.

Her name was Rabbitt, with two t's. I liked her smile. I liked her tool belt. I liked how her tool belt looked natural on her. Then I saw her eyes. Cupid's arrow embedded itself. I began to flirt outrageously. She seemed oblivious. Another lost cause. I sighed.

She asked me what I did for a living. I told her that I was a librarian and a teacher, working on my thesis for my MLS. She smiled and said she had just finished her MA in English. Jackpot. A woman with power tools and a graduate degree. I was glad I had made no promises to Mary. My flirting began to take a serious turn.

I was called away for other work on the ground level. I did not see Rabbitt for a while. When I did, she was with the other woman. The woman in the passenger seat of the Galaxie. Were they friends or lovers? The $64,000 question of the day. No one seemed to know. I backed off...some.

I wrangled my way into the cutting crew, which consisted of Rabbitt and me. I held the plywood while she cut roof sections with a circular saw. She needed a pencil, and I made her retrieve it from my breast pocket while I made sexy, off-color comments. She remained oblivious. I flirted ever onward.

The wood chips flew into her eyes as she cut. We stopped and looked in vain for goggles. I offered her my glasses, prescription glasses for a rather bad astigmatism. She handed them back with a laugh, saying the lines were too wavy. She looked at me, and suddenly her expression changed. I thought she recognized me and maybe I had done something awful to her sometime, somewhere, that I couldn't remember. But she smiled and helped me to heave the boards onto the roof. She even snarled at my ex-girlfriend, who offered to help. That was promising.

But there was still this other woman to contend with. Who was this stranger, and why was she with my woman and in my Galaxie? I took a hold of the reins of my emotions and stiffly pointed out to myself that Rabbitt was not my woman and that was not my car. Yet.

Finally the work was done. The crew sat around an open fire, drinking beer and eating leftovers. Rabbitt was discussing a deck she wanted to build and asking the forewoman for advice. I quietly offered to help and gave her my number. Rabbitt looked amazed and asked if I was willing to drive all the way to Las Cruces from El Paso to build a deck. Inside I was screaming: *Of course I would, you fool! But who is that woman you're with?* I nonchalantly answered, "Yes."

I waited two weeks for a call, lamenting my fate. Then she called. I was casual, calm, collected. "Yes, I can be at your house on Tuesday. Sure, no problem." Then I hung up and made a screaming call to Mary. "Who is that other woman?"

Mary said to maintain my cool. The woman must be a friend. Why else would Rabbitt call? I wasn't sure. Tuesday was taking too long to get there. They didn't act like lovers. Maybe they were friends. They didn't even look like they were together at the concert I saw them at together. Maybe friends…lovers…no…friends. This was beginning to sound like a *Cathy* comic strip. I told myself to shut up and not count on anything.

Tuesday…Las Cruces…I rang the doorbell. There was Rabbit with her tool belt and no one else but me to work on the deck. Jackpot. I could live with this one. And I do.

The Park Bench

BY CONNIE JEWELL

Lesbian. There, now that I can say the word, what do I do about it? Now that I accept who I am, where and how do I find others like me? I tried the bars, but that wasn't for me. They were a foreign country, with strangers speaking an unintelligible language. Events crystallized around me as if I were a wispy apparition. Solitude was preferable to another foray into that jungle.

Hmm…how about the personal ads? Now there's a thought. You don't have to be drop-dead gorgeous to hold someone's attention long enough to interest them beyond the physical. Well, I had no idea how radically my world would change from just placing a $5 classified ad.

The final draft of my creation read: "What A Deal! GWF, 29, creative, intelligent, witty, spontaneous, caring, and good-humored, with interests in movies, art, books, music, and weekend trips. ISO mature, stable GWF, 28-36, with similar interests and qualities for friendship and possible relationship. I'm looking for someone who enjoys an occasional night out at the clubs but whose world does not revolve around it." So I put a stamp on the envelope, placed it in the mailbox, and hoped for the best.

Only one week after the ad appeared, responses started rolling in. I excitedly read and reread them all. However, one particular letter kept luring me back. There was something about it that was familiar, so warm and safe. So all I needed was the nerve to make the phone call.

Maybe a drink first. There, OK, I've had a drink. Now take a deep breath and dial the phone. O-o-oh…ring…ring. "I'm sorry, I can't come to the phone right now, please leave a message after the beep."

Wow, that was a close one. But I get to leave a message and then she has the enviable duty of starting the conversation when she calls back. Yeah, this is easy, so far.

Two days and three rounds of phone tag later, we finally spoke for the first time. It was 10 A.M. on a Sunday morning. I remember I was basking in the August sun on my deck that morning, sipping coffee as we spoke on the phone.

The conversation wasn't nearly as strained or awkward as I expected. At once comfortable and natural, the conversation flowed. My nervousness fled, and all thoughts about the gravity of my actions disappeared. I forgot that I was making my first actual date that evening with a woman. A woman! Oh, what had I done?

Time jumped into hyperspace mode that afternoon. Before I knew it, the time for my date was upon me. Date! What was I thinking? As I decided what to wear, applied my makeup, and got dressed, I kept saying to myself, *I can't do this.* Amazingly, the thought went through several stages. The *I can't do this* mantra became *I'm going to throw up,* then, *I am going to do this.* Finally, realizing that I wanted my many fantasies to become reality, *You must do this* won out over the others.

The 30-minute ride to the restaurant was a blur. Somehow I materialized in the parking lot in front of Chili's restaurant. Compulsively, I was early. I walked in, but "mystery woman" had not arrived yet. Will she even show? How long should I wait? Why am I the only single person in the waiting room? Shouldn't she be here by now?

Then she walked in, breathless and a little frazzled. I later learned she had suffered a flat tire en route to our meeting and barely made it.

I was really nervous. Not so much around Vicky—yes, she had a name and everything!—but by knowing I was finally "living the dream." The thought gave me an adrenaline rush.

In a flash an hour and a half passed. I knew we had to leave, but I didn't want the date to end. Outside the restaurant I asked Vicky to take a walk with me. I was pleasantly surprised when she accepted the invitation. We walked a bit, then found a vacant park bench.

I was in a near-hypnotic state. We talked for another two hours. I couldn't hear her voice enough. It was low, smooth, and sexy. It captivated me completely. If a late August thunderstorm hadn't come in suddenly, we would probably have sat on that park bench all night. Neither of us wanted to part from the other.

But the storm won. I went home and couldn't sleep. Over the next week eating and sleeping became fond memories. Thoughts of Vicky filled my being. I wanted to know more about her. I wanted her to get to know me. And as much as the thought frightened me, I wanted to know what it would be like to touch this woman and feel her touch me. I wanted to know what it would be like to look into her soft green eyes, kiss her lush lips, then lose myself in her. There was such a bond that I felt we had been together before, on some level, in some paradise.

Looking back, I can't remember what my life was like before her, and I can't imagine my life without her. After seven years together, I still want to sit on that park bench with her all night and hear her low, smooth, sexy voice tell me every dream and wish she has for our future together.

What a Deal!

BY VICKY WAGNER

For too long I had lived like a vampire. Doomed to wander the night, cut off from the warmth and love of others. I was lonely, empty, and in need of companionship. The soft glowing skin and loving smile of a mortal woman was just the thing I needed to bring me back to life.

So where does one search for such a creature? Not the bars. I had done that scene and been disappointed on more than one occasion. And I knew all of the friends of friends who could possibly exist. This too was a barren field. The one area of possibilities remaining was— drum roll, please—the classified section of the *Baltimore City Paper*.

As chance would have it, I stopped for a paper on just the right day. The planets were aligned and all was right with the universe. There in the middle of the second column was the ad. "What A Deal!" read the heading. And after reading the description of her, I had to agree. She too was not interested in spending every waking hour in a bar. We had like interests and goals. I just had to pursue this. I mailed my response that night—no delay here! And within a week we made first contact by phone.

Her voice was soothing to my ears. Though we had never met, I felt as if I had known this woman before. We agreed to a meeting that evening at Chili's restaurant. Six P.M. sharp.

As I parked in the lot across from the restaurant, myriad thoughts played across the screen of my mind. What would she be like in person? How could such a prize still be available? Would she even show? In only minutes I would know these answers.

A rush of cool air struck me as I pushed open the front door to the restaurant. There she was, waiting. My mind was so overloaded with impressions and feelings that, to this day, it is difficult to delineate my thoughts. But I'll try.

Most immediately I realized this was a very attractive woman. The kind of beauty one can be comfortable with and worship from up close, not at an awe-inspired distance. As we walked to the table, with me behind her, I noticed she looked great from that angle as well. This had definite possibilities!

As we conversed, I was pleased to learn that she had a fine mind and a great sense of humor too. Wow! Looks, brains, and personality. Amazing. And she was nervous. At meeting me! And I was worried that she would find me uninteresting.

I knew I should do something to make a favorable impression. Something daring. Then I remembered that during our phone conversation, she had described herself as "average-looking." Here was my chance to appear gallant, tasteful, and smooth all at once. I was in the zone!

"You know, Connie," I said across the Caribbean salad. "You lied to me on the phone today."

From the look on her face I knew I had her wondering. Nervously she asked what I meant.

"You told me you were average-looking," I said, pausing for effect. "That isn't true at all. You're very pretty, far above average."

Pow! She loved it. A good impression, and I had let her know I thought she was hot, but in a nice, tasteful way. I had the moves, baby!

If anyone missed it up until now, I offer this clarification. I was all but blown out of my seat by Connie. I felt I wanted to spend forever with her. Not just a lifetime, but longer. Such good vibes emanated from her. And we talked so easily. Yet I was every bit as nervous, on the inside, as she appeared on the outside. I did what I did purely to avoid having our ships pass by in the night.

The amazing thing is that seven years later, I still have those same feelings about her. After a year-long courtship, I moved into Connie's apartment. It was all so natural. Her parents accepted me as a member of the family—Thanksgiving and Christmas dinner, occasion cards to their "other daughter."

And I find that my first impressions were correct. Connie and I are best friends who can talk about anything together. I prefer to spend time with Connie because I like her, as well as love her. She is a beautiful, sexy woman with all the intellectual qualities I find interesting in a woman. If I had to sum her up in one short phrase, I'd have to say, "What a deal!"

Madeline's Version

BY ANONYMOUS

After I came out to my friend Mary, she asked if I'd ever been in a gay bar. I hadn't, so she made plans to take me to a local gay bar. I was nervous, afraid of running into people I knew or might know me. Mary asked if an old military buddy of hers could come along. I was having problems dealing with my newly discovered self, and Mary thought her friend, Lou, might be a good person to talk with. Lou had lived both gay and straight lifestyles. I thought she would be old and boring.

I was still at work when they came to pick me up. When I looked inside the car and saw Lou, it felt as if someone had squeezed my stomach. I was instantly embarrassed because she was attractive, and my reaction took me by surprise. I didn't look at her. I drove home and changed my clothes, scrapping my original dowdy outfit. I put on something I thought *she* would like.

I sat in the backseat behind Lou. I could only see the back of her head. I talked to Mary mostly. If I had been facing Lou, I wouldn't have been able to speak at all. When we reached the bar my feelings of nervousness resurfaced, and I was afraid to go in. But when Lou smiled, I forgot all my fears.

Inside, I bought a round of drinks. Mary talked, but I wasn't really listening. My eyes scanned every face inside the bar. I was shocked to see so many women from softball. Luckily, no one I knew very well.

Mary encouraged Lou to tell me about her experiences. As Lou talked I could only watch her mouth. One of her front teeth was the tiniest bit longer than the other. I was mesmerized by her mouth. I don't remember a word she said.

I really liked her, and I felt like I could look at her forever. But I thought there was no way she would be interested in me, because I was almost 20 years younger than she. I knew I would dream about her that night.

At one point I commented about the women dancing, and Lou, knowing I was still nervous and scared, jokingly asked me to dance. I figured this would be my only chance to be close to her. I couldn't let it pass. We danced a slow dance. My whole body felt electrified and excited, and I couldn't help but wonder how she felt. She whispered in my ear, "I wish I could make love to you right now." I was scared spitless, but I managed a smile. I thought it was a compliment, sort of.

We returned to the table, and the electricity between us set up a force field no one could break through. We were only focused on each other, not hearing or seeing anyone else around us. Lou left to go to the rest room. Realizing we could have more private time together, I followed after her.

Outside of the rest room was a recessed area in the wall, open on one side, closed on the other. We reached the area at the same time, and I grabbed her and kissed her. We kept kissing, unable to control ourselves. A group of women heading into the rest room whistled and hooted. Several minutes later they came out. We were still kissing, and they went wild.

One woman pulled us apart and held our faces together. "When did you meet?" she asked.

"Tonight."

"Don't they make a cute couple?" she asked her friends.

They all agreed we did. We went on kissing for what seemed like hours. Finally we returned to the table, dazed and elated. The bar was closing.

During the ride home we sat in the backseat together. I leaned into the front seat to talk to Mary. Lou rubbed my back. I caressed the inside of her thigh.

After we dropped Lou off, Mary warned me against getting involved with her. I wasn't really listening. I was too busy thinking about the woman I had just met and wondering if she would really call.

She called.

Lou's Version

BY ANONYMOUS

Madeline and I have been together for five years. Some might not consider five years long-term, but everyone we knew was certain we would never make it this far. Ours is an intergenerational relationship with 17 years' difference between us.

We met three months after I retired from the military. I contacted Mary, an old friend, and she told me about a young woman she had befriended. Madeline was having a difficult time accepting her sexuality.

Mary invited me to attend her softball games. I noticed one member of the team sitting in the bleachers, her neck in a brace. She had a definite baby butch look; her hair was cut close to her scalp. Mary told me the baby butch was Madeline.

I went with Mary and Madeline to a local gay bar. Mary wanted me to talk to Madeline because I had experience with both straight and gay relationships. We drove by Madeline's workplace, where Mary formally introduced us. I thought Madeline was cute, but bashful. She seemed nervous.

After we picked her up, we drove to the bar. She slid into the booth across from me and ordered two beers. I joked, kidded, and flirted with her. She smiled a lot and seemed to relax. We drank and talked for hours. Maybe I talked and she listened. I felt as if we had known each other for years. I felt a strong attraction toward her, but I didn't think she could be attracted to me.

Jokingly I asked her to dance, certain she would say no. But, to my surprise, she agreed. When the music slowed I pulled her close. We were the same height and fit together perfectly.

"I'd love to make love to you," I whispered, emboldened by the beer.

Finding a dark corner, Madeline kissed me. A long, passionate kiss. The first of many.

When we returned to the table Mary was angry, making sarcastic remarks, and during the drive home, she didn't say a word. In my folks' driveway, Madeline gave me her phone number and kissed me good-bye. I repeated the number over and over. I thought about her all night. My stomach flipped as I remembered her kisses. I repeatedly argued with myself about calling her, uncertain about getting involved with someone so young.

I called.

The Mary and Merril Show: Part I

BY MERRIL MUSHROOM

I heard about Mary B-J long before I ever set eyes on her. "Have you met the new woman in town?" the counterculture folks all asked me. "You really should—the two of you have so much in common." So much in common meant she was a dyke (so was I), she was from New York (I wasn't, but I had lived there for almost a decade before moving to my present home), and we both had biracial children. No doubt she heard about me too, but we just didn't connect; we would be at the same places but at different times. I was curious about her but not especially interested. My life was full.

Then I went to the coffeehouse...

"Let's go into the city Friday," said my friend Kay, "and live it up for the evening." The city meant Nashville, 75 miles away. Live it up meant going to the monthly women's coffeehouse and dyke fest.

"Sure," I agreed. That Friday evening, I got myself up in my go-to-the-city butch outfit—lavender Cuban lace shirt under red overalls—and applied a dab of scented oil to my neck, took pains with my hair, got into the car with Kay, and off we went. I was into doing some serious cruising at this event, even though I had a lover. She lived 500 miles away, and we were not monogamous.

The coffeehouse was held in the meeting hall of a church on a hill. One could enter through the upstairs wing into an open vestibule, which afforded a good view of the entire room below.

One could scope out the scene before descending the staircase into the meeting hall. This one did so, studying the women gathered below. Kay disappeared into the ladies' room. My heart warmed in sudden pleasure when I spotted my dear friend Jo, sitting at a table with another woman. Jo looked up, saw me, waved. The woman looked up too. I didn't know who she was, had never seen her before. I looked harder. She was beautiful, very hot, even from that distance. I wondered if Jo was dating her, felt a strange pang of jealousy at this thought, wondered at this feeling, and felt ashamed, wished Jo well with this very attractive woman. Jo was motioning me to come over. Eagerly I descended the stairs and crossed the room to where they sat.

I slid into the chair at the front of the table between the two of them, greeted Jo warmly, smiled at the new woman. She was even lovelier close up, had an incredible aura about her that I much later learned was her natural intensity enhanced by PMS—but, oh, goddess, it was so attractive then. I mumbled something inane to Jo about not wanting to interrupt her date.

"Oh," Jo giggled, "we're not dating. This is Mary B-J. She's new in town."

That was Mary B-J? The woman I was supposed to meet for so long? Suddenly I felt shy, awkward. I turned to Jo, made small talk. "So…how's your life been?"

"Boring," Jo replied. "How's yours been?"

"Boring," I echoed. My mind was empty of brilliant repartee. "Hmph," I said, blandly, "nothing like another boring conversation."

"Excuse me." Mary B-J stood up and walked away from the table.

Jo and I looked at each other. I shrugged. Might as well take advantage of her absence. "So tell me all the poop you know about her," I demanded. "I'm glad you're not dating her."

Jo told me what little she knew, encouraged my interest—and I was interested. But Mary stayed gone. Jo got involved in another, no doubt less boring conversation, and I got up and wandered the floor for a while, chatting with dykes I hadn't seen in ages. Then I caught sight of Mary B-J standing by the staircase. Casually, hurrying without seeming to, I made my way over to her.

"Hi," I called.

She glanced at me coolly, nodded.

I cornered her against the steps, tried conversation again. "So, I hear we both lived in New York at the same time. Where did you hang out?"

"Kookie's," Mary replied with the name of an "uptownie" bar. "Where did you hang out?"

Little did I know at the time that she would sooner have stayed home than go slumming at places like the Sea Colony, or worse, Washington Square. "Mostly the Sea Colony, but sometimes I'd go to the Washington Square," I replied in complete ignorance. Mary looked away. "Every now and then," I continued, "my buddies and I would go up to Kookie's and cruise the snobs." I chuckled. "Usually ended up going home with them too."

Mary looked back at me again, cleared her throat. "So what were you?" she asked. "Butch or femme?"

What? I drew myself up to my full 11 feet 8 inches, leaned back slightly, arched one eyebrow. "Need you ask?" I drawled. "And you?"

"Oh," Mary looked up, coyly. "Femme. Femme, of course."

"So," I continued, "I hear you're in a long-distance relationship."

"Yeah," she nodded.

"So am I. But we both date, and my lover has another lover, and so does her other lover. How about you?"

"We're monogamous."

"Oh." I was a little disappointed. She was really attractive. But I try to be easy to get along with. "Well, if you ever decide to date, let me know, OK?" I ventured.

Mary glared at me. "We'll see. But I don't think so. Excuse me."
And she turned around and walked away again.

I didn't see her anymore that whole night.

In the car on the way home, Kay told me she had made this great
connection with Mary B-J, the new woman in town.

The Mary and Merril Show: The Real Story

In the spring of 1981 I was smitten in New York City by a woman who, shortly after we met, was transferred to the South. I put the word out that I would be interested in work anywhere in the Southeast and was soon offered a one-year contract at a regional university in Tennessee, only a 2½-hour drive from my intended's new home. Two weeks after I turned in the U-Haul, however, it was pretty clear the relationship was probably not going to survive the year.

I decided to have an adventure. Following the bulletin board trail, I met Connie and Jo, and they introduced me to dozens of women from Nashville and from the surrounding communities. I was particularly interested in country dykes at the time. Lots of people, even straight people, kept telling me that I just had to meet a woman named Merril. Not only did she live out in the hills, they said, but her politics were compatible with mine. In fact, Merril represented "the next wave of the women's liberation movement," they said. But I kept missing her at parties and concerts, and I hadn't yet met another adventurer either. Then Connie and Jo suggested that I cruise the monthly women's coffeehouse. They said Merril would likely be there too.

The coffeehouse was held in a church that was perfect for cruising. Entering from the upper parking lot, one passed the office and meeting room on the way to an open area overlooking the nave, the site of the main activity. Here one paid the modest admission fee, taking one's time to see and be seen from below. Particularly brave or brazen women could step over to the low wall by the stairs and study the scene before descending. With Connie and Jo on either side, I did just that. I learned from my coaches who was available, who wasn't, who just might be; who had good politics, who had kids, who was closeted, who was bi, who claimed to be straight. Nobody immediately interested me.

"Is Merril here?" I tried to sound casual. She wasn't.

We descended the stairs and took up a position at the end of a long table in the middle of the room. Connie and Jo sat opposite each other at the end of the table closest to the "stage" area, and I sat next to Connie. Within five minutes Connie said she would be back and went off to campaign for something. As she left, I scanned the room.

"Jo," I gasped. "Who is that stunning woman on the stairs?"

"That's Merril!" she squealed, gesturing the woman over.

The Legend approached, resplendent in her red overalls and lacy lavender shirt, swinging her arms and bobbing her head ever so slightly, looking clear and confident and, well, very sexy. Nothing in my body, neither small muscles or large, would move in the desired direction. I wished for an out-of-body experience. Before it could happen, though, she was at the table, greeting Jo. She wasn't looking at me, but the angle of her head and body said she wanted to. Jo introduced us at last.

"So you're the famous Mary B-J!"

"And you're the famous Merril!" I said, thinking, *Oh, gosh, where to go from here?*

Blessed be, the music started. Since Merril had slipped into Connie's seat, and we all turned to face the performer, I was seated slightly behind Merril and Jo, and I had a good chance to wink at

Jo and check out Merril. She was indeed stunning. There wasn't anything notable about any one feature, but the aggregate was breathtaking. She was tall, very much taller than I, but she was not imposing. She was so self-assured and easy. I found that both intimidating and very, very attractive.

The music stopped and we applauded. I held my breath. Merril didn't move. I decided to say something to Jo, mostly to help me relax. I leaned slightly into the space between Merril and Jo.

"So, uh, what can you tell me about the singer? I like her sound."

Just as Jo began her reply, Merril leaned sideways toward Jo, her back still to me. "So how was your week?" she boomed.

"Boring." Jo was still facing me, but turned slightly to reply to Merril. "And yours?"

"Boring." (Pause.) "Just what you need to close out the week. A boring conversation."

Jo chuckled briefly, then turned to me, apologetically, I thought. But I was already gone...into my thoughts. *So! That's the new wave of the women's liberation movement! Rude! Now we're going to be rude to each other. Groovy.* I needed space.

"Excuse me," I said and left for the refreshment table. I ordered white wine. As I waited for my drink, a woman with a splendid voice spoke to me from behind.

"You're the new woman at the university. I've been dying to meet you—as is everyone else in town. Hi. I'm Kay. I really do want to talk to you. About Women's Studies and such. How 'bout we go outside and get stoned?"

I remembered I had promised myself an adventure. "Sure," I said answered, then followed her out to the parking lot. In the car she rolled a joint with one hand while she fumbled for the lighter.

"Do you see the lighter? This isn't my car. Drat."

"I have matches," I said, producing them. "Whose car is it?"

"Merril's. She's my neighbor out at the Creek. We came together, but we're not an item. Awesome woman. Met her yet?"

"Yes," I said, editing my reply with huge slashes. "Interesting woman."

Kay and I talked a long time, mostly about feminist politics, her
being bi, life on the Creek, and the women of the greater Nashville
area. If I was doing it with bi women, I would have been interested
for sure. I could settle into an easy friendship with her, however, and
I planned to do so.

Returning to the room, I stood at the bottom of the steps, feeling
mellow and scanning for new women. Suddenly she was upon me.

"Hi!" said Merril again. "I hear we both lived in New York at the
same time. Where did you hang out?"

"Kookie's." Was there any other appropriate place? "And you?"

"Mostly the Sea Colony, but sometimes I'd go to Washington
Square." I tried to conceal my reaction, lest I be rude, too. Those
bars were full of riffraff, biker dykes, stone butches, rough trade,
mols, and "het wanna-bes." All threats to the stability and re-
spectability of the community. And outrageous. Intriguing. Sexy.
"Usually ended up going home with one of them, too," Merril was
saying.

My curiosity was swamping my judgment. "What were you?
Butch or femme?" I asked.

She drew herself up to her full 11 feet 8 inches, leaned back slightly, cocked her head, arched an eyebrow. "Need you ask?" she invited.
"And you?"

"Oh, femme. Femme, of course," I lied.

"So. I hear you're in a long-distance relationship," said Merril.

"Uh, yeah." Actually we were in stage three of a seven-stage
breakup, but "yeah" was good enough to keep the conversation
going with a huge escape hatch.

"So am I. But we both date, and my lover has another lover, and so does her other lover. We're nonmonogamous." This was the denizen of the Sea Colony talking. Seamy. Rough. Apolitical. Not into committed relationships. "Do you date?"

"No," I said from the door of the escape hatch. "We're monogamous."

"Well, if you ever decide to date, let me know, OK?"

"We'll see," I said. Was she making fun of me? The downtown butch did that sort of thing. And made being rude a high art. "But I don't think so." Then I walked away without a word.

In the car on the way home, I thought about the evening, about all the neat women I was meeting in Tennessee, about her. I didn't want to think about her, but there she was. She was not imposing. Just present.

A Divine Decision

BY JANET L. GRAHAM

It was a two-hour drive from my hometown to my new dormitory at the university residence. I had the whole summer to consider what my future might hold as I left my family and my dogs for the big city, but mostly my mind had latched onto trivial worries about whether I would be "allowed" to wear jeans to class, whether I would be issued a locker on campus, and what changes might have been made to my lecture schedule. I was still very much in my high school mind-set.

For someone so obsessive and independent, I was remarkably untroubled by the prospect of sharing a tiny dormitory room with a total stranger; I experienced no sense of foreboding whatsoever about my unknown roommate. While friends fretted about being saddled with some wholly unsuitable, I remained sanguine. Far from feeling anxious about the living arrangements that would soon rule my life, I was much more concerned with how I was to haul around mountainous piles of textbooks and binders from building to building. I had an instinct about my roommate, whoever she might be—a strong, firm conviction that we would get along well.

I was the first one in the room that day and had already ascertained from the nameplates taped to our door that the other occupant's name was Rita. This unlikely, old-fashioned moniker unnerved me slightly—I had never been friends with a Rita. Inside my Spartan new home, surrounded by cartons filled with my clothing, study aids, and carefully transported stereo, I shooed away my ever-helpful parents, crushing my mother's hopes of staying around to greet my new roomie. I had no desire for an audience. I wanted to acclimate myself to my surroundings and practice appearing at ease and likable for the moment when Rita crossed the threshold. But first I chose the best bed and largest closet.

With hovering relatives dispatched and all vestiges of my past receding from my thoughts, I began to unpack and soon met one of the girls from the adjoining room. She was, even to my unsophisticated eyes, obviously a dyke—loud, friendly, but visually unappealing, easy to spot, and perhaps just as capable of placing me, an unsettling idea, since I preferred to remain charmingly nondefined in my orientation. I had moved to Toronto to study, period.

Shortly thereafter I met the girl who would reside in the friendly dyke's room and hence also be a suitemate of mine. She was, as it happened, a longtime friend from my high school. Sister Diane, the nun who ran the nominally Catholic girls' residence, evidently believed that, as hometown familiars, this friend and I would enjoy sharing a washroom and the short hallway separating our rooms. I couldn't decide if Sister Diane was right. In any case, two of my three fellow residents were in place, though Rita still had not arrived.

In anticipation of her entrance, I mentally reviewed my coexistence strategy; above all else I required that my roommate accept and endure the two grand passions of my life: the Bee Gees and the Toronto Maple Leafs. If only she could put up with the fraternal harmonies and twice-weekly hockey games, I was prepared to make whatever concessions or accommodations she deemed necessary.

Finally she appeared. The clamor at the doorway caused me to turn away from my stereo-connection duties to catch a glimpse of the girl I would be living with. Oh, no, she was wearing a dress! And her baggage cart was overwhelmed by a giant stuffed animal. My roommate was a femme! She said hello, but did not introduce me to her mother—a young woman with extravagant hair and too much makeup. Rita and this woman placed the over-sized teddy bear on the floor and set down a few other things, then left to retrieve more boxes from the elevator. Alone again, I used the time to consider my plight.

What on earth could I have in common with a prissy little girl like that? Should I ask Sister Diane to find me another roommate? Should I query my hometown friend about exchanging roommates? Should I defer my panic until this new girl and I had actually spoken to one another?

When Rita reappeared with the last of her belongings, she explained that it had been her Toronto–based sister, not her mother, who accompanied her and that she too was from a small town, even farther north than mine. In unaccented English she revealed that her primary language was actually French and that she intended to pursue a career in…psychiatry. What a coincidence. So did I! Only later did we realize that our similar professional goals had surely prompted the dean of residence to assign us together, but at the time it seemed uncanny.

Rita started to unload her personal effects, including all manner of academic trophies and plaques—awards for excellence in calculus, French, physics, and chemistry. I was so impressed. It was such luck to have an intelligent, accomplished roommate, someone who might tutor me through impenetrable maths and sciences I was obliged to study. This was a coup.

I possessed no equivalent badges of scholastic glory, but fervently wished to demonstrate my own seriousness, so I scrambled to unearth highly graded essays of years gone by, hoping to dazzle her with copies of "*King Lear* and The Book of Job: A Comparative Study,"

"Prejudice and Discrimination," and "Hitler and the Rise of Nazism." She expressed interest in them all.

It took little time for me to appreciate how Rita was easy to talk to, how pleasant, sincere, and unaffected she was. I fell immediately "in comfortable" with her. Our rapport was so genuine that I could speak more candidly and intimately with her than I had ever spoken with my mother or my best friend. This compatibility seemed entirely natural, and others in the residence took to calling us "the twins" due to our constant companionship and (slight!) facial resemblance. From our first meeting, talking with each other became a necessity, taking precedence over sleeping and certainly over studying.

Seventeen and a half years later I feel the same necessity and the same sense of completeness I have known since the day we met. In truth, Rita and I are two complementary beings whose aspirations, ideals and affinities are neatly synchronized, and yet, if left to our own devices, we might never have met, as the superficial differences in our personalities would have made us unlikely friends.

Luckily our fates rested with a certain Catholic sister who read through scores of residency applications and somehow perceived the possibilities. God only knows how she would regard the outcome of this intuition of hers, but as Rita and I stoically cheer on the Toronto Maple Leafs and relax to our 30-disc Bee Gees collection, we remain grateful that she was so inspired.

Janet

BY RITA MASCHERIN

I still smile when I remember the first time I met Janet.

It was our first day at university. I was a shy, 18-year-old, small-town French Canadian moving to the heart of the largest city in Canada. I didn't know what to expect, and I was nervous about meeting the roommate who would share my small dorm room.

I wore a white dress, wanting to look my best, although in retrospect it seems like an odd choice for moving day. With my older sister behind me, I walked in and saw Janet for the first time. She was wearing a blue hooded university sweatshirt and tight-fitting blue painter jeans. Unlike me, she seemed so cool and collected as she assembled her stereo and casually greeted me. I haven't the foggiest idea what we said to each other in that first minute.

In the time I went downstairs to fetch my clothing, I forgot her name—it was short, something simple like Karen, yeah, Karen, that was it (she's never forgiven me for this).

Back in her presence, I was awed by her personality. Janet was so articulate and sure of herself. She was amazed that I spoke French and rushed to the next room to share this information with a home-town friend. She then took out her wallet to show me what looked like a magazine cutting of two small dogs, which she said were hers. I thought she was joking, of course. But eventually I found out the photo was real, taken by her photographer father.

I didn't know what to make of this person. Half the time I had no idea what she was talking about. She kept going on about the "leafs" (I always thought it was "leaves"). It took me a while to figure out she meant the Toronto Maple Leafs. Who knew that a 19-year-old girl could be a rabid fan of a professional hockey team? I liked hockey too, but I hadn't really watched it since I was a kid. Janet was unlike anyone I had ever met.

That night we went to eat with the other newcomers. Janet seemed to want to tag along with me, as much as I wanted her to. She actually seemed to like me even though I had done nothing to impress her—after all, she was the impressive one.

When I went to visit my boyfriend two weeks later in another city, Janet's name kept crossing my lips. I couldn't wait to find out what she thought, what she did, if she missed me, although I never would have asked. I mean, it wasn't like I was, you know, that kind of girl. I didn't think so anyway. Well, maybe I was bisexual, but that was irrelevant. It's just that I liked her a lot.

We could talk about anything. We could stay up until 3 in the morning confiding our deepest thoughts, even with 9 A.M. classes to get to. And she was so funny, although I didn't understand her sense of humor. I found her incredibly intelligent and verbal. She had opinions about everything—sports, politics, education, music—and was never at a loss for words.

When, 2½ months after that first day, Janet told me she loved me, my heart leaped, and I melted into her lips. I had never known the meaning of love before. No one else has mattered since.

Or Words to That Effect

BY TANYA HUFF AND FIONA PATTON

Fiona:

I first met Tanya in 1985 when I was living in Toronto. I was a somewhat young 23, working in a lumber mill and trying to manage the elusive discipline needed to write a book. Tanya was working at Bakka, Toronto's science fiction bookstore, and had already managed it.

Friends of mine and I were in the habit of walking down to Bakka about once a month or so. This day was warm and sunny, and I noticed Tanya at the counter for the first time. She was blond and capable-looking, and I remember thinking how pretty she was. I wanted to casually strike up a conversation with her without looking like an idiot. Not an easy task when confronted with "first impression panic." I think I babbled some semiwitty, semilame remark about needing to move the store closer to the subway because it was a long way to walk.

She smiled.

Whether she smiled out of the tolerant boredom that most retail people reserve for irritating customers who think they are funny and original, or not, I can't say, but she didn't make a disgusted face, so that was good enough for me. At that point my friends were ready to go. Rather than ruin a halfway decent first impression, I moved on.

Tanya:

When you work in a popular store in the downtown core of a city of three million, so many people come and go that it's almost impossible to remember individuals until you've seen them over and over again. But I still remember that first meeting with Fiona.

She was wearing a military-style bomber jacket and a baseball cap, and had masses of gorgeous dark hair. All right, so I wasn't certain if she was a girl or a very pretty boy (she looked about 16, top estimate), but since I assumed she was merely passing through my life that didn't affect a purely aesthetic appreciation.

I remember that she seemed nervous, and I thought that was pretty cute.

Fiona:

Within the next few days I was invited to join a Toronto-based writer's group. Two of the members were already published authors, and so with awe and trepidation I found the apartment and was introduced to the eight other members.

One of them looked familiar. She was blond and capable-looking and pretty. I think I said something brilliant like, "Have we met?" We had.

Tanya:

Now, I was really pissed off when I heard there was a new member coming into the group. First, because we had set a limit of seven members, which we had already reached. And second, because I was one of the two founding members, and no one had bothered to mention it to me until after it was settled.

When I saw who the new member was I calmed down a little. I remembered this person from the store and I realized two things. One, it was definitely a woman. Two, she had absolutely beautiful green eyes.

The first time she read a piece for the group, I was amazed by the power in her writing.

Fiona:

All through that summer and autumn, whenever the group met Tanya and I sat next to each other. I know this because we have the photographic evidence. It wasn't planned, it just happened over and over again.

Tanya:

Actually, it was occasionally planned. I'm not very comfortable around most people, but sitting or walking next to Fiona felt so right I arranged to do it as often as possible.

Fiona:

One evening while I was listening to another member read, I was sitting on the floor at Tanya's feet and wanted to lean my head against her legs, a physical step forward, which would have been totally innocent if I hadn't already been smitten. So, screwing up my courage, I did it. She casually reached down and ran her fingers through my hair.

It was a great summer.

Winter came. I was living at my parents' house that year, an intolerable situation I was anxious to remedy. One of the other members of the writing group mentioned that Tanya was looking for a roommate. So, once again screwing up my courage, I called her and said, ever so casually, "I hear you're looking for a roommate."

She said, "No, I was wondering if you were."

Or words to that effect. Romantic panic coupled with disbelieving relief tends to blur actual dialogue. And after a week or so (a small amount of time that seemed like an eternity), I moved in with her, complete with a room full of books, a cat, a pack-a-day smoking habit, a handful of rowdy friends, and two relationships.

Despite all of this, Tanya (a rather more retiring person than I am) did not kick me out.

Tanya:

I had just gotten rid of a disaster of a roommate and was making enough money that I didn't financially need another. But I was lonely, and there was only one person I could see myself living with. A little shy of approaching Fiona directly (which should have cued me in about my actual feelings), I mentioned I had an available room to a mutual friend, allowing Fiona to come to me.

When we sat down and started talking about it, it didn't matter that she had a cat (I had three) or that she smoked (as long as she did it in her room) or that she was involved in two relationships.

The day she moved in, one of those relationships came with her and I found out that it did matter. A lot.

Fiona:

So time passed. Not a whole lot of time, granted, but some time; about eight months as I recall. I liked her. I really liked her. And not just as a friend. I remember looking in the bathroom mirror and thinking, *Aw, crap, I'm falling in love with her. What could she possible want with me? I couldn't be that lucky.*

Nonetheless, before one of my opportunistic, but socially shy, friends could maneuver between us, I once again screwed up my courage (I had to do a lot of that). One night at bedtime I walked to her door and said, in the dark so she couldn't really see me, "I have something to tell you and you probably already know it, but I have to tell you anyway that I really like you and I'm really attracted to you but you're probably not interested in me but I hope you are and you feel the same and if you don't I'll understand."

Then I ran.

Again the wording might have been different; I hadn't paused for breath long enough to let oxygen reach my brain. I do remember her response, though.

"Get back here."

And so it was decided. We would go slow, but we would go.

Tanya:

I had assumed that I was putting out all these intense, "I really like you and I'm attracted to you and now it's your move," messages. I ran around in my underwear a lot, but it didn't seem to have much of an overt effect. We had a lot of intense conversations, and we had so many of the important things in common. I knew this woman was someone I could spend the rest of my life with, but fearing rejection, I waited for her to make the first move.

When she finally did, I didn't know if I was more relieved or terrified.

Fiona:

Eleven years, a wedding, two car wrecks, a house, six cats, a dog, and umpteen manuscripts later, we are still together. I still get nervous hoping she will like me, and I still have to screw up my courage. Only now it's because I spent too much at Canadian Tire or because my mother wants to come to visit. We are an old married couple, either potting about the garden or watching the television. But we still sit next to each other and she still runs her fingers through my hair.

Tanya:

I'm still afraid of rejection, but not so much that I can't, occasionally, make the first move. We live comfortable lives and we talk about absolutely everything. No, really, absolutely everything. And did I mention she had gorgeous hair?

alyson books

AFTERGLOW, *edited by Karen Barber.* Filled with the excitement of new love and the remembrances of past ones, *Afterglow* offers well-crafted, imaginative, sexy stories of lesbian desire.

DREAM LOVER, *by Jane Futcher.* The enduring power of adolescent fantasy tempts one woman at an emotional crossroads in later life.

EARLY EMBRACES, *by Lindsey Elder.* Sexily sizzling or softly sensual stories explore the first lesbian experience for women.

THE FEMME MYSTIQUE, *edited by Lesléa Newman. Women's Monthly* says, "Images of so-called 'lipstick lesbians' have become the darlings of the popular media of late. *The Femme Mystique* brings together a broad range of work in which 'real' lesbians who self-identify as femmes speak for themselves about what it means to be femme today."

HEATWAVE: WOMEN IN LOVE AND LUST, *edited by Lucy Jane Bledsoe.* Where can a woman go when she needs a good hot…read? Crawl between the covers of *Heatwave,* a collection of original short stories about women in search of that elusive thing called love.

THE LESBIAN SEX BOOK, *by Wendy Caster.* Informative, entertaining, and attractively illustrated, this handbook is the lesbian sex guide for the '90s. Dealing with lesbian sex practices in a practical, nonjudgmental way, this guide is perfect for the newly out and the eternally curious.

THE PERSISTENT DESIRE, *edited by Joan Nestle.* A generation ago butch-femme identities were taken for granted in the lesbian community. Today, women who think of themselves as butch or femme often face prejudice from both the lesbian community and the straight world. Here, for the first time, dozens of femme and butch lesbians tell their stories of love, survival, and triumph.

PILLOW TALK, *edited by Lesléa Newman.* Climb into bed with this collection of well-crafted, imaginative, and sexy stories: an unbridled celebration of lesbian eroticism. These tales simmer with intrigue, lusty encounters, and lots of hot sex between the sheets as well as some other creative places. These spicy stories will leave you begging for more!